ALTERNATOR

A biased guide through the world
of alternative music videos

(1990-1994)

Alternator
A biased guide through the world of alternative music videos (1990 – 1994)
Rasťo Kachnič et al.

© **self published by Rasťo Kachnič**

Author © Rasťo Kachnič
Authors of chapter '1994' © Rasťo Kachnič and Julian Duckworth
Commentaries to the music videos © Rasťo Kachnič,
Mark Sherrington, Braňo Špirk, Adam Nenadál, Robo Vehner,
Kubo Magál, Ivana Klučková, Julian Duckworth
English translation © Mgr. Eva Eddy, PhD.
Proofreading of English translation and Consultant © Jonathan Eddy, M. A.
Photography by © Rasťo Kachnič
Graphic design and typesetting © BcA. Milan Pleva
Printed by: Amazon KDP

First English edition (2022), 256 pages

ISBN 978-80-570-4432-1

Contents

ALTERNATOR

A biased guide through the world of alternative music videos

(1990 – 1994)

Rasťo Kachnič et al.

2022

Preface

This book is about experiencing music rather than about 'reading about music'. In it, you will not find interviews, band profiles, or reviews. This book strives to entice you to actively discover, listen, watch, and share.

For many music lovers, what they could see on their TV screen in the early '90s thanks to MTV was a small cultural revolution. Videos and artists (whom present-day critics would most likely label as 'alternative') who appeared in the given era in daily rotation or could be seen in such night-time programmes as 'Alternative Nation', 'Headbangers Ball' or '120 Minutes', might not find their way into the scheduling of music channels at all nowadays. Together, they formed a great genre mix of rock, hip-hop, punk, electronic, metal, and their mutual combinations, thanks to which, today, the '90s are remembered as a decade when no genre crossover was considered impossible. Luckily, now there are other ways to watch music videos and we are not merely reliant on the offer of TV music channels, as a great number of these exquisite forgotten or underrated videos and artists can be found online.

We have dug through the archives from 1990 to 1994 and carefully selected for you 333 songs by over 250 artists. We tried to give you

333 good reasons why we got to like this period and, at the same time, provide you with the output of the most influential and most popular musicians (from the 'world of alternative music') in the first half of the 1990s. For company, they have a broad selection of indie artists releasing on respected independent labels, one-hit wonders, clever copyists, and anything and everything in between. The selected songs can be ordered from essential to obscure; here, hits are just as likely to be found as forgotten compositions, and personal favourites occur side by side with generally recognised pieces. We hope some of them catch your eye, grab you by the ears and, perhaps, touch your heart. You might remember songs you have not heard for a while or, even better, you will get excited by something you have never known before.

It was not our interest to create a compilation of 'the best of the first half of the 1990s'. This book is not an encyclopaedia which includes complete discographies or videographies; nor is it a complex collection of songs you 'should listen to before you die'. It should serve as a springboard for your further discoveries. We tried to portray the amazing musical diversity of this period in the history of music with all its contributions, key new musical trends, and genres linked to it. Nevertheless, space is also given to momentary and unsuccessful experiments, or dead ends. Among over 300 albums from which the videos for this book were selected, some timeless classics can be found as well as some genre milestones, which should not be left out of any music fan's collection, together with hidden gems, unrecognised geniuses, as well as guilty pleasures. Since everyone's music taste is very subjective, personal ratings of the albums are passionately diverse and biased. It is, therefore, truly up to your discretion into which category you will place the individual albums.

We also wanted to pay tribute to the format of the music video. In early '90s, videos came to be an extremely popular and effective tool for the promotion of music. In many cases, a spectacular video played a key role in bringing the artist to light and drawing the attention of fans as well as the music media. Some videos alone acquired iconic status and became recognised cultural phenomena. There is no recipe for a perfect music video. A countless number of approaches to the right ratio of picture and sound provides an exciting insight into the personality and creative vision of the artists. When filming a video, some authors based it on the lyrics of the song and used it as a motif for a story; others focus on enticing shots from a concert; some enjoy being seen in the video, while others prefer to hide from the public. Some decided to invest a ton in the video's making, while others were happy enough using their loose change; some tried to impress with a deep message, others stood out with their crazy side. All this and much more can be found in this book.

So, discover, listen and watch, and should you get to like something that you have heard and seen, share it. Go to concerts of your favourite artists, buy their albums or T-shirts. Or, at least, tell someone about them.

Methodology

— The book only includes songs for which an official video was made and released or broadcast in some way.

— The introductory text of each chapter only includes references to bands and artists who, during their career, filmed at least one video. If more detail is provided about a specific album, there is at least one corresponding official video to be found.

— The videos are divided according to the years when the album with the respective song was released, while the single or video version of the song might have come out in a different year.

— The chapter 'Index of included albums' provides a list of all the recordings to which closer attention is paid in the accompanying text or their video is commented on in one of the chapters. The list also includes complex information about the release of the album (artist's name / album title / year of release / record label / name of video). All this in case you would like to get it from your favourite music supplier.

— The year of release and record label refer to the first release of the album on the national market. This information might differ if the record was released in various countries or on different formats.

— The maximum extent of the accompanying texts about the videos is 320 symbols (i.e., approximately two text messages) with the aim of briefly and aptly presenting the song. We express the reasons why we like the piece, hoping you will also get inspired. All texts were originally exclusively written for the music blog 'Alternator' between 2012 and 2015 and they are presented here with the kind permission of their authors.

— The limit of 320 symbols refers to the text written in the native language of its author. Translation into another language might have exceeded this limit.

— On some pages of the book, there are QR codes with a link to one of the videos commented on – this was done so you can check out straight away what you have just read about.

— QR codes refer to videos from the official profiles of the artists and their record labels. By watching and sharing them, you increase their visit rate and, at the same time, their chance of being rewarded by the streaming company.

— At the time of writing this book, all QR codes were functional. This, however, might have since changed. Also, some links might be unavailable due to geographical restrictions. We are, therefore, sorry if something is not working but there is very little we can do about it.

Introduction

In order to understand the value of the videos and their impact on '90s music fans, it is important to realise how different the world was before the internet was available for the masses. Try to imagine your day without social media, when you are not able to reach your friends by chat, share your opinion on a discussion forum, or simply send an e-mail.

Forget about torrents and downloading data files; you can but dream of listening to an album without actually owning it in some physical form. The most accessible music-related souvenir is an A3 poster on the wall of your room, while a T-shirt with the logo of your favourite band is a sacred garment.

The websites of your favourite artists and record labels are not yet in existence; you cannot search for news in online magazines, nor can you read a review on a music server. There is no Wikipedia, no Pitchfork, no Allmusic, no RateYourMusic, but mainly, there is no Youtube, or even Dailymotion or Vimeo. There is really nothing. What opportunities, thus, did music fans have when they wished to find out what was going on in the world of music?

To find where there is an upcoming concert next Friday, all we needed to do was check the lamp posts, underpasses, and bus stops in certain parts of town for posters. Do not forget there was no internet browser available, which means there were no Citylife-like websites; there were no Facebook invitations we could unearth and share on our walls. Posters were, thus, an irreplaceable tool for concert promotion.

We could also stop at a local record store and take a leaflet promoting a tour, pop into the right pub, where those 'in the know' would hang out, or glance at the noticeboard by the toilets. When an unknown band came to town, you could not check out their profile on Bandcamp and listen to their newest album, nor skim several pieces on Soundcloud to find out whether they are 'worth' seeing. If the poster said it would be a punk band, we simply had to hope they would play the specific type of punk that would kick ass. The only way to find out was to go and experience it first-hand.

At the concert, fans were likely to encounter someone selling fanzines, often written by hand and released in a limited run. They did not merely include profiles, reviews, and interviews with bands, but also the addresses of independent distributors from whom you could get such titles that a sane record store owner would not even stock by mistake. All you had to do was send a letter with extra stamps for the return postage and, in a few days, you were holding their distribution list. Back then, we did not have Discogs to hand and good old 'snail mail' was the fastest way to communicate with sellers outside your hometown. Naturally, you could also take a bus and see them in person.

When a music fan at the beginning of the '90s wished to follow the trends, wished to discover new bands that had just broken through or simply wanted to find out something about interesting national and international scenes, it required a bit of effort. The best and most reliable source of information of the time were music magazines. Those who grew up in the USA definitely did not miss the latest issues of 'Alternative Press' or 'SPIN', British fans, on the other hand, leafed through 'NME' or 'Melody Maker'. Here in Slovakia, if you were lucky, you could read some of these magazines in a library, in the department of foreign press; however, it was easier to make peace with the offer of the local issues and nip in the closest newsagent's and buy 'Rock & Pop' or 'Bang'.

Still, would you buy an album just because someone gave it a good review? Or would you buy a ticket to a concert merely based on an interesting interview with the band or seeing their picture in a magazine? Especially when you are a teenager, and you have to think twice what you spend your pocket money on. No description can replace the sound experience; the opportunity to listen to at least a sample is key in such a decision-making process.

Nowadays, you can commonly find samples of songs embedded directly in reviews on music servers; you can have the exclusive right to listen to entire albums on the day they were released; news subscribers can even find pre-release tasters sent directly to their inboxes before the pieces officially come out. Today, we are able to find anything in a few seconds – all we need is a few clicks with the mouse. In the early '90s it was nowhere near this simple.

Naturally, the first place where music fans could hear the new trends was the radio. Even those listeners who had not grown up in a country where John Peel's legendary broadcasts on the BBC could be caught, they could at least try to tune into the local students' radio and, in this way, enjoy a little bit of adventurous alternative to the common commercial broadcasts.

Radio was an excellent source of new music; together with a blank tape slid in the door of your cassette player and your finger ready on the 'record' button when a promising song started to play. At the turn of the '90s, tape was still the most sold sound audio carrier, even though it was soon to be steamrollered by a massive increase in the popularity of CDs. To buy the 'original cassette' was, in those times, as common as buying a digital download in the present day. Blank tapes were the only readily available medium on which one could make a copy of an LP, CD, or, possibly, a radio broadcast. From the recorded songs, we could do selections and listen to them over and over, also in the car where cassette players reigned for a few more years.

When we wanted to share the new discoveries with our friends, we could not just send a link to Drop Box. You simply had to meet them in person. Armed with cassettes and, later, CDs, we threw listening parties where we were trying to outdo each other with our latest discoveries. Meeting and sharing was a significant part of every music adventure.

Every week, we went to the local record store to listen to the new albums that were played there for the very first time. The owner of the shop knew us as his regulars. He recommended new releases we might like and passionately talked about the pieces that had just come in. He kept complaining about people having bad taste and his poor sales. Once, however, he noticed a friend of mine sadly staring at the CD he badly wanted but could not afford, as he had already bought another one that month. The owner knew we were students with empty pockets, so he asked him whether he would be OK to pay half price. When the friend shyly nodded, without a word, he took the CD off the rack and shoved it in the box with discounted goods pretending it had been there forever and walked off to the counter. Even though he was a businessman, he was primarily an avid music enthusiast and understood where we were coming from.

Those of us more interested in underground records unavailable in regular shops could try their luck at the nearest punk concert with the hope there might be an 'independent distributor', a weird guy with a crate full of LPs and CDs. Should we not like the album we bought, he promised to give us our money back if we were to catch him at the next concert.

Sometimes we happened to start chatting to the concert pro-moter, excited by the bands playing on the night and he would promise to lend us a few LPs we might like, even though he did not even know our names. He trusted we would come next time and return them. These stories would most likely not happen these days. Thanks to the technological possibilities, music has become so readily available that similar gestures of solidarity or the honest will to share are, suddenly, somehow unnecessary.

Before the era of the wide availability of home internet, the world was a much smaller place, which meant music also reached us in smaller doses. Every acquired record was an event, as getting it took considerable effort and/or the spending of precious pocket money. Original records were not cheap and we really had to think twice before we bought them. It meant buying a pig in a poke, as there was no option to stream it and listen to it beforehand to make sure we would like it.

It was due to these overcome obstacles we appreciated music so much. If we did not like a record straight away, we gave it a second, or even a fifth, chance and listened to it again and again. We knew each piece in detail, as we had heard it multiple times, until we got under its surface. Thanks to that, we had a chance to better understand it, experience it, and get attached to it. In today's fast era, there is no time for that. We are flooded daily by new music and it is more and more difficult to just sit down and listen to the entire album undisturbed. We need to keep checking the news feed, respond to our friends' statuses, or reply to messages in chat.

Thanks to the advances in information technology, there are barely any obstacles to overcome. Music is available at the click of a mouse in any conceivable format. We do not need to leave the house, we do not need to risk, conquer music, or look for a key to it. There is so much of it everywhere that, should we not like an album, we can simply turn it off and play something else. Music has become available for literally everyone; it has, however, lost some of its magic. Listening to it is no longer an exceptional ritual of discovering but rather a daily routine.

Even though we had enough information from magazines and the radio to be able to get to and exchange a lot of exceptional music, there was still something missing. As they say, better to see once than hear a hundred times, and this also applies to big music names. To get at least a taste of their personality and experience their radiation, it is also better to see them than just read about them or listen to them.

The best way to connect the names of our favourite musicians with their faces was to 'park ourselves' on the couch in front of the TV screen and turn MTV (Music Television) on. Watching it was a perfect replacement for hanging around the music shop window, which resulted in dream lists of records we really needed to get or concerts we really needed to attend one day.

MTV was our YouTube of the 1990s. All it broadcast was music, videos were on all day, 24/7. In the broadcasting structure of those days, there were no series, reality shows, or documentaries about the lives of music celebrities. Also, there were not as many channels thematically based around various music genres.

An everyday mix of videos was interlaced with short blocks of music news and entries by VJs introducing the new videos. The stream of music was also interrupted by trailers for newly released albums, ongoing tours, or one of the genre-specific programmes; with commercials being given minimum space. The only exception were the crazy and smashingly original idents of MTV itself. Simply said, MTV at the beginning of the '90s was exactly what it said on its label – music television.

Even though MTV, from its very foundation in 1981, was more focused on the listeners of mainstream pop-rock radio, it also very willingly stretched its ears outside this comfort zone. Thanks to that, it was able to react to the current events on the music scene and did not hesitate to confront its viewers with more progressive and, for the time in question, more adventurous pieces than simply the work of well-tested stars.

Just like in the 1980s, it reflected the increase in popularity of the new wave of dance groups, in the years to come it gradually provided space to rising waves of hip-hop, grunge, Britpop, or pop punk. Especially in the first half of the '90s, when it did not fully realise its immense marketing potential, MTV was a place where one could feel honest interest and verve for music and music videos, almost regardless their genre and time of release, which was also reflected in its music scheduling.

MTV brought its viewers a colourful mix of new and established, trendy and classic, presented with a healthy batch of boldness and the ability to enthuse. In the nightly genre specials, it also remembered the fans of metal, alternative or dance music; it presented recordings of concerts and music festivals. It started a successful and respected series of unplugged performances; every year it rated the best videos and gave them awards at galas called 'Video Music Awards'; it gave birth to the animated metal fans Beavis and Butt-head, and many more.

Put simply, MTV was fun, up-to-date, exciting; it had style, and it was hard to change the channel once its logo settled on your TV screen.

For many fans it was MTV that was the gateway to musical events worldwide. It was also the first map to find your way in the genre jungle and a key to understanding music connections. Videos were one's first contact with a band or a solo artist. We discussed them at school during breaks and whoever missed the current hot topic of debate had no other choice but come home, turn the telly on and patiently wait till it is on again.

For some of us a well-made video was a reason to hunt for other records or more information, for others an impulse to go and see their first concert. Many a decision to finally take a musical instrument and learn how to play it, or start a band, was made in front of the TV screen. It was only thanks to music videos that some realised what hairstyle they wanted to have.

If you are holding this book in your hands, it might be that a music video has left a major trace in your life and you will remember it on one of the following pages. However, if you only reached for it out of curiosity, one of them might just be here waiting for you.

1990

Public Enemy

Living Colour

Alice in Chains

New Model Army

Sonic Youth

Cocteau Twins

Happy Mondays

The Charlatans

Iggy Pop

Ice Cube

Midnight Oil

Morrissey

Mother Love Bone

Depeche Mode

Jane's Addiction

1990

By the first year of the 1990s, all those factors that were to play a key role in the upcoming earthquake in the music industry had gradually moved in the right direction. Music charts and commercial radio stations were still a safe place for 'easy' listening, ruled by smart looking pop stars and musically smooth production was dominated by the sound of keyboards as the legacy of the previous decade. Nevertheless, the change was round the corner, ready to jump out with noisy vigour. Those key ingredients that helped to turn the music world upside down did not appear out of the blue; they had been around in various forms for years. They lived their own happy lives, aside from the interest of the popular press and radio waves, perfecting their abilities and patiently acquiring the attention of those who wished to listen to something fresh and exciting. Let us have a closer look at what that year brought about outside the direct interest of the common radio listeners and the majority of the music-buying public.

In the USA, hip-hop not only proved its viability but also commercial potential as early as the late 1980s. Come the next decade, it was not flogging a dead horse for sure, either. On the contrary, it was in excellent condition, brimming with ideas and exploring various artistic approaches. Many significant representatives of the genre reached their creative peak; their lyrics focusing on various topics, from biting social criticism to political commentary. Rappers definitely excelled in creating inventive, complexly structured rhymes, as well as ways of their presentation, while producers drew from a bottomless well of samples ranging from jazz to funk, and from rhythm and blues to rock'n'roll.

In 1990, *Public Enemy* strengthened their reputation of politically engaged rap monster with their third record *Fear of a Black Planet* and built an undying monument to the art of sampling, for several generations to come to draw from. *Ice Cube* abandoned his former gangsta rap 'crew with an opinion' and started his solo career with the album *AmeriKKKa's Most Wanted*. The record became an instant hit, never lowering the platinum bar he set with any of the following albums released in the 1990s. *LL Cool J* managed to win back his street cred when he changed his mind about the pop ambitions indicated on his previous record and, instead, bared his claws again belligerently when he released *Mama Said Knock You Out*.

Hip-hop was just experiencing its golden age and, even though its peak was still to come, it already was experiencing significant support in this era in the form of the show 'Yo! MTV Raps'. Every week, rap fans could not only see newly released videos but also interviews with the main stars of the genre as well as live performances. This programme significantly contributed to the spread of hip-hop music and culture worldwide. Many a rapper started to write their first rhymes thanks to MTV and, perhaps, until the present day, carefully stores in the cellar videotapes with recorded clips that he used to hone his flow.

The main worldwide rock scene seemed to be firmly held by glam metal bands, which enjoyed the turn of the decade at the peak of their popularity. Nevertheless, so-called 'alternative rock' was also slowly becoming to be known. For the time being, it was hiding in local music scenes, mainly patronised by the schedulers of student radio, reviewed by underground fanzines, and followed by enthusiastic fans of subcultures but, even these side stages of rock music were alive and filled with great and splendid bands. Major record companies started to realise this too and tried to fish in such waters where only independent labels used to operate.

They might have been encouraged by, originally, punk rock heroes *Hüsker Dü* or the darlings of student radio stations *R.E.M.* successfully entering the world of major labels at the end of the 1980s. Either way, 1990 brought about further transfers of originally independent artists to the first league of music. After a decade of pioneering balancing between regular songs and eruptions of noisy guitar feedback, *Sonic Youth* deservedly won the respect of their fans and the recognition of critics. Thus, with an offer by a major label they were given a chance to confront a larger audience with their new release, *Goo. Jane's Addiction* recorded an impressive follow-up to their first big budget record and, with *Ritual de lo Habitual,* reached a whole new level of epic rock pomp. The growing rumours of a distinct music scene from the American Northwest based around Seattle were to be confirmed by *Mother Love Bone.* They were the first band of the local underground to sign a contract with a big label and their debut *Apple* was expected to be quite something. Their singer, Andy Wood, however, died suddenly, only a few days before the record hit the shelves. Expectations were dashed; and yet this was to be only one from a whole line of premature deaths of significant talents framing the musical story of the 1990s. He, thus, did not live to see the events that were, in a few months, to make his home of Seattle the centre of world music events.

On the other side of the ocean, on the British Isles, exciting times were also being had. From the end of the '80s, music periodicals had been competing in coming up with superlatives to describe bands from the Manchester area. These, in their works, combined rock progressions underscored by dance beats. They drew inspiration for this new, until then unheard of, sound from the psychedelic '60s and an important role in the increase of its popularity was also played by the increasing availability of ecstasy in the area. The scene in which the rock club and dancefloor fused on one stage got to be called 'Madchester'. Even though most of the bands on this scene exclusively released their records on an independent label, they dominated not only the British indie charts but were also in the top positions of the official singles charts at the turn of the decades.

Their popularity culminated in 1990. With their *Pills 'n' Thrills and Bellyaches, Happy Mondays* brought their celebration of life in the form of a 24-hour party to perfection. On their first album *Life, Inspiral Carpets* resurrected the psychedelic sound of the Farfisa and, in the studio, immortalised the compositions they had played live several months before on John Peel's programme. The debut album *Some Friendly* by *The Charlatans* became the first and only Madchester record to conquer the top of the British album charts in spite of the fact that they, paradoxically, did not come from Manchester.

Nevertheless, the greatest stars of the scene were, undoubtedly, *The Stone Roses*. Even though they did not release an album in 1990, they made sure their fans remembered them thanks to the single *One Love* and, especially, the legendary concert at Spike Island. Although it was, primarily, they who claimed to be the best band worldwide, the over 25-thousand strong audience that came to see them that night would have surely agreed.

The roots of traditional British 'indie pop' are to be found as early as the beginning of the '80s. Back then, the musical underground rocked with the rumble of post-punk characterised by sound exploration, experimentation with various genres and, oftentimes, bold composition structure. Singles charts were dominated by synth pop groups celebrating the possibilities of keyboard progressions. The inclination towards more simple and melodious guitar songs can, thus, be perceived not only as a natural reaction to artistically ambitious, albeit, oftentimes, listener-demanding, post-punk production, but also the dehumanised electronic sound of synth pop. Indie pop bands followed the tradition of British music of the '60s, with an emphasis on catchy melodies and a clear, jangly guitar sound. From the current events, they primarily acquired enthusiasm and the 'do it yourself' punk approach. As a result, they did not overly worry about their musical abilities and felt more at home on the turf of independent record labels, or they even founded their own. It was also from this breeding ground that several prominent faces were to pop up only to shuffle the order of the British music charts.

In 1990, after long months spent in the recording studio, the perfectionists *The La's* finally managed to finish their first eponymous album. Back then, they surely had no idea that not even after 30 years would their fans still be waiting for a follow-up. There was no shortage of beautiful melodies on *Reading, Writing and Arithmetic*, the debut LP by *The Sundays*, whose light guitar songs won the hearts of loyal fans, especially in the USA. After a series of successful singles released in the previous months, *Morrissey* decided to put them together on a compilation. The outcome was named *Bona Drag*, which, until the present day, is considered by aficionados to be one of the peaks of this contradictory master of verse, always ready to start a public debate with an apt statement, or leave a considerable part of his concert earnings at his hairdresser. Those who like to sing along while listening to the radio would definitely be in their element.

In spite of their limited recording and marketing budget, these were usually independent record labels releasing inspiring and innovative music. They were not primarily driven by the pursuit of money; instead, they possessed enthusiasm, creative vision, and a passion for music that encouraged them to also discover and release such artists who valued originality more than commercial success. They were often placed in an environment of emerging subcultures and local scenes, and in the background of fresh genre trends before they were taken over by the music industry and transformed in its own image.

In the first half of the '90s, 'independence' came into fashion and, suddenly, money was to be squeezed out of it. Big record labels, thus, founded and financed offshoots and used independent distribution channels, with the aim of making their new acquisitions more visible in this market. By contrast, independent labels entered into ownership and distribution partnerships with big companies in order to allow wider availability of their artists' records at the national or international level. As a consequence of these activities, the term 'indie label' was devalued and it was hard to know which label was just a branch of a big company, or which of those that had always been independent preserved their independence and to what extent.

In spite of that, many classic indie labels kept going for years and made history. If it was not for their bold searching, we would have been poorer by a great number of fantastic records. Even though they had gone through various mergers, changes in ownership, share issues, and even bankruptcy, they still managed to rise from the ashes to go on and spread the music they believed in.

The British label 4AD was established in 1980 by Ivo Watts-Russell and Peter Kent, at that time employed by Beggars Banquet, a well-known indie label of the day. A year later, Ivo Watts-Russell became its sole owner and, at the same time, a music visionary. When selecting artists, he avoided contemporary musical trends, being more interested in the artistic dimension rather than the commercial potential. This approach of his was emphasised by his close cooperation with the designer Vaughan Oliver, who created special graphic designs for the majority of the catalogue items of the label in the first 15 years of its existence. Together, they managed to combine uniqueness of sound and impressive images and, by their perception, raise music from a consumer product to a work of art.

Among the most prominent figures of the mid '80s appearing in their catalogue were such ethereal bands as *Cocteau Twins*, *Dead Can Dance*, or *This Mortal Coil*. The dreamy and mystical atmosphere and personal depth of their recordings lay the foundations of dream pop and defined the typical 4AD sound of this period. Instead of repeating a proven concept, they expanded their publishing scope in the second half of the decade, when they also looked into the American underground. Their first catch was *Throwing Muses* with their post-punk drive, and 1990 already caught 4AD successfully rooted not only on home soil, where they released the dreamily melodic *Lush* and *Pale Saints*, but also across the ocean. From there, the increasingly popular *Pixies* appeared in Europe with a new release, *The Breeders'* debut was still considered to be a side project, and *His Name Is Alive* proved that dream pop had taken over in America as well. By the end of the 90s, when Ivo Watts-Russel decided to completely leave the music industry, he had also discovered for us, with his label, the painful beauty of *Red House Painters*, the carelessly seductive *Belly*, or the sleepily smooth *Mojave 3*.

His inspiring twenty-year tenure with 4AD, as well as the wealth of timeless music he helped bring to the world, was paid tribute to by the journalist Martin Aston in the extensive biographical book *Facing the Other Way: The Story of 4AD* (2013). Fortunately, his departure did not mean the end of the label. To this day, 4AD are among the leading independent labels and persistently explore musical fields outside the mainstream.

In the 1990s, the availability of music videos from independent artists on television screens was not great. One option for those who had a video player at home was to get one of the music compilations on a VHS tape.

That year saw the release of three instalments of the excellent *Indie Top Video* series following the best of the UK indie chart with videos by *The Soup Dragons*, *Depeche Mode*, *James* and many others. Creation Records boasted the best of their catalogue. Their collection, not the most creatively named *The Creation Records Compilation*, featured, among others, the trio of sound innovators *My Bloody Valentine*, *Ride*, and *Primal Scream*, which was soon to determine the events on the domestic music scene. The American label *Amphetamine Reptile* worked harder for a fitting name not only for the name of their label, but also for the *Dope-Guns' & F*cking Up Your Video Deck* compilation. Samples of early work by *Cows*, *Helmet*, and *Tar* became a valued artefact for all fans of noise rock. Such subheadings as *"Loud-Raw!!! Obnoxious!!! Even Naked!"* are some shining examples of the promotional material telling the complete truth and the fan getting exactly what they paid for.

Still, the simpler option was to rely on television. Even though MTV had not yet ventured into too much experimentation during daytime broadcasts, fans of minority genres could rejoice every Sunday at 1 o'clock in the morning.

It was around this time that the two-hour programme called '120 Minutes' began, mapping the sounds of the musical underground. The best of post-punk, gothic rock, and synth pop of the '80s, as well as Madchester, indie pop, and much more, was 'served up' every week by the British VJ Dave Kendall to all those who found this dose of 'different' music worth staying up for to the early hours. That is, unless they were the lucky owners of a VCR and were able to record the programme. Even though the programme mainly focused on events on home soil, echoes from across the Atlantic were also given space, so there was no shortage of alternative rock, nascent industrial, and even pioneering crossover bands of the time crossing rock with rap, funk and other genres.

Despite the obvious minority representation in its broadcast structure, from 1989 on, MTV has reserved one category for alternative videos in its annual program MTV Video Music Awards, initially called 'Best Postmodern Video', but only two years later the award was renamed to 'Best Alternative Video'. This also gave fans of 'diverse music' a reason to sit in front of the telly and watch MTV giving awards to the best music videos of the year.

MTV does not consider a calendar year as the evaluation period for its Video Music Awards. The jury select from videos broadcast no later than mid-June of the current year, which meant that the majority of the videos still were released during the previous year. As a result, many of the videos nominated in 1990 were released in the 1980s, which was also reflected in the choice of the performers. It was not only the awards given to the best videos, but also the live performances of selected artists that were a big attraction of this musical event. The musicians actually performed live, so in many cases it was a unique opportunity to see such bands and performers in action whose concerts you would not have otherwise been able to attend. This also often resulted in the broadcasting of unexpected moments.

In 1990, the best of dance pop, hard rock, glam metal, mainstream rap, and pop that had been born in the past twelve months took turns on the stage and, if not for one exception, it would have been a representative sample of mainstream radio broadcasts of the time. The one act that stood out from the rest was the all-around epic *Faith No More*. Their dynamic mishmash of funk, metal, and rap, the bizarre costume of Mike Patton, who seemed to have grown an extra arm that night, and also the spontaneous stage performance of the whole band seemed in the context of the evening as a visit from another world. After their show, which ended with a provocative allusion to a video clip that raised the blood pressure of animal rights activists, many viewers were most likely wondering what the heck they had just seen. Yet, thousands of others had just discovered their new favourite band.

Nevertheless, the main event of the annual MTV Video Music Awards is still the announcement of the awards for best music videos. Although the prize is usually accepted by the award-winning performers, the success of the clip also goes to its director. In the early '90s, the music video format was still exploring its possibilities. Rather than an artistic statement, the videos were often just crafted accompanying images that served a simple purpose - to transfer a song from the airwaves to the television screen. However, as MTV grew in popularity and influence as a music medium, videos began to attract more and more talented creators and directors. This was soon reflected in an increase in the quality and artistic ambitions of the works created.

Many a director, nowadays well-known from the film or advertising industry, began their careers by directing music videos and, in contrast, quite a few renowned directors were happy to find time for a few clicks of the clapperboard to the rhythm of their favourite band's music. All those who devoted their creative energy to the artists of the nascent alternative scene contributed their bit to the musical revolution of the '90s. Thanks to them, it was an inventive revolution, bursting with creativity and the discovery of new possibilities for combining image and music.

Depeche Mode was among those nominated in the 'Best Postmodern Video' category in 1990 for the song *Personal Jesus*. Despite the fact that the best years of synth pop were over by then, it was their then new record *Violator* that made them into world-class stars.

The Dutch photographer and director Anton Corbijn was in charge of the visual representation of all four singles from the album. He began his career of more than forty years by taking pictures for the British music magazine NME in the late '70s, impressing the readers with his suggestive black and white images. Over the years, he captured the faces of such artists as *Tom Waits, U2, Cocteau Twins, Jeff Buckley, Pearl Jam, Nine Inch Nails* or *Siouxsie Sioux*, many of whom have appeared on the covers of renowned magazines or album covers. An impressive selection of photographic works documenting his obsession with music was published in a profile book entitled *'Anton Corbijn – 1-2-3-4'* (2015).

In the '80s, he successfully established himself as a music video director. He especially got to like *Depeche Mode*, for whom he has shot more than twenty video clips to date, but *Metallica, Mercury Rev, Johnny Cash, Rollins Band* or *Nick Cave and the Bad Seeds* also turned to him with confidence. Anton Corbijn was not afraid of the big screen either. In his brilliant debut, *Control* (2007), a biopic about the singer Ian Curtis of the legendary *Joy Division*, he used his knowledge of the musical landscape and black-and-white imagery to perfection. He, however, also proved to be good when working in colour and within the spy thriller genre in the film *A Most Wanted Man* (2014).

Even though his video did not win the prize at the 1990 MTV Video Music Awards, he made up for it four years later, when the jury awarded *Heart-Shaped Box*, which he shot for *Nirvana*, the best alternative video of the year. Although, in recent years, he has mostly been busy with feature-length productions, he still pops off from time to time to shoot a music video. So far, he has done more than 70 of them and, hopefully, he still has a few ideas left.

The following pages feature video clips shot in support of singles released in 1990.

Selected and commented on by:
~ Shezz, + Zebra, # Aran, * Rasťo, ° Iva, × Kubsson,

Sonic Youth - Dirty Boots   *

"Each Sonic Youth album is the best," Milan said as he lent me "Goo". The very first song was the best one. It was my inauguration into the world of amazing intuitive song structures, where the solo doesn't have to follow after the second chorus and guitar feedback is used as another instrument; all that in the background of the world's most romantic video.

Mother Love Bone - Stardog Champion   ~

Whilst this song isn't the catchiest on the album, the video is a great example of MLB and the era. A loose premise of a video interspersed with live and backstage footage. After Andy Woods' death, critics praised his style of interacting with MLB fans as 'the only stand-up comedian front man in Seattle'.

New Model Army - Purity

I have probably listened to this song more than any other in my life. "Impurity" was the first New Model Army record I became familiar with – and this 20 year long relationship is still lasting until the present day. Everything is totally beautiful about 'Purity': melody, lyrics, and even this reasonably pathetic video.

Cocteau Twins - Iceblink Luck   +

E.T. dropped his musical hardware over Scotland. Intentionally. He helped to create music from another planet. Incomprehensible, and perhaps that's why the ethereal, vibrating voice of an angel, accompanied by a soft caressing bass and cuddly synthesizer, will take you to a world which is soothing and irritating at the same time. Only you can choose which it will be.

The Soup Dragons - I'm Free   *

I do not usually sparkle with enthusiasm when listening to cover versions. But I applaud when somebody can make it so good that it sounds like their own. It was objectively not Soup Dragons' fault that some band called the Rolling Stones borrowed their song 25 years before. That's why they just, naturally, took it back. Especially when they are allowed to do what they want…

Jane's Addiction - Been Caught Stealing   *

People have various hobbies. Some play in a band, others like to dress in freakish costumes, several are happy when stealing something. Somebody got the idea to put it all together and this dotty video was created and, in the lyrics, Perry Farrell managed to ironically describe today's reality of the music industry 20 years in advance.

Ride - Vapour Trail ~

A two-minute song with a two-minute outro, yet with deep lyrics, still works well. 'Ride' introduced me to the genre of what was to become 'Britpop', but they did not compete*. The video, which could now be made on any home PC, was actually made by scratching and damaging the film cells to create the effect!

Nick Cave and The Bad Seeds - The Weeping Song °

If Cave's lyrics are reflective insights into the darkest places of man's psyche, then the music of the Bad Seeds is their identical music twin. Here, both are lightened by a paradoxically humorous video where Nick can even be seen laughing spontaneously! Because even this dark gentleman knows that darkness will be replaced by light, and if he weeps, it won't be for long.

LL Cool J - Mama Said Knock You Out +

A psychopathic maniac who wipes the whole world out like a storm, and that is just the warm-up round. Raw and very pissed off old school rap. LL Cool J spills his funky rhymes and is, at the same time, ready to beat up anybody who crosses him. And when his mum says to "knock you out", he will not hesitate. Nobody answers their mama back, homie.

Iggy Pop - Candy   +

The godfather of punk tamed by a redheaded diva in the most romantic song of his life! A conversation of a couple, divided not only by distance and the scents of their new lives, but also an age gap of twenty years. However, their memories pave a solid road to the moment when they discovered their closeness. So that later, thanks to separation, they could find an undying love.

Fields Of The Nephilim - For Her Light   *

A gloomy wayfarer came out of heavy fog wallowing in the valley. An amulet is hanging on his chest, and he carefully keeps scrolls with mystical writings in his satchel. He has cold, steely eyes and his face doesn't remember how to smile. He hasn't always been a troubadour of darkness, as he used to have love in his heart. But only the obituary remained.

Happy Mondays - Kinky Afro   ~

How should you feel seeing a guy in a band do nothing but a kind of induced dance? That's the dilemma many had. But watch this without; it's just not the same. A classic song and video that put them on the map, and an inspiration to the many bands that followed and cited them as 'ground-breaking' in the genre.

Living Colour - Type

Yes, they had mad trousers, disastrous shirts, and stupidly painted guitars, but Living Colour were a great band in their day. Especially their record 'Stain', which delivered. I used to call them 'Bad Brains for the mainstream' and I really dug a couple of songs – like 'Type' with a massive guitar riff and sweet chorus.

Depeche Mode - Personal Jesus +

The church is waking up. A mass of incense stalks of dark blues is smouldering. Its smoke is burning inside my nose, making my eyes water, and soothing my hot-tempered mind. Thanks to a cleansing bath, I can now more clearly see the face filled with my own expectations. I know the depths of persisting desires and the shallow nature of spontaneous craving. I reach out and touch faith – in me.

The Charlatans - The Only One I Know *

Hard work and will sometimes matter more than being original or coming first. From the beginning, they were written off as Madchester sounding epigones and candidates for the title 'One Hit Wonders'. In the end, they have survived all the fickleness of the music audience as well as personal tragedy and enjoy well-deserved respect today. Here is that first 'one hit'.

Fluid - Black Glove   *

They had the right volume, the reputation of being a live attraction and just about the right amount of garage dirt on their guitars. But, as the saying goes, "they cried well, just on the wrong grave". At the time of the birth of grunge, lively rock'n'roll was celebrated, instead of introspective darkness, and they forgot to buy some fashionable flannel shirts. Thus, fame passed them by, but they were actually rather good.

The La's - There She Goes   ~

Mike Myers enjoys a Scottish accent, but before Shrek and Austin Powers, he done possibly his best work, and this is the theme to that film*. It has a happy, upbeat, feel good vibe, which is a pop-indie rarity. Almost a one hit wonder, but not quite. However, when the La's split up, we then got Cast, so every cloud…

Midnight Oil - Blue Sky Mine

A genius of a song by one of the best pop bands of all time. It gives me chills EVERYTIME I hear it. I think that a song like this can only be written by somebody once in their lifetime – not more. The only sad thing here is that Peter Garrett in his later years became exactly the thing which he protested against; especially with this song…

Jane's Addiction - Stop!   +

A punchy hit from a breakthrough album, where Perry Farrell shows off his surfing and stage skills. A bit of magic powder backstage and let's hit the sun-soaked stage. Below him, there is a boiling pit full of surfers eager for the energy of sea, sun, and storming riffs, and even some for the powder backstage.

Deee-Lite - Groove Is In The Heart   *

I do not believe that anyone ever dreamt of this becoming a hit. It has too much craziness to be calculated. Rather, this song and its video is a flower child born of a successful party and a free-minded brainstorming session. Loopy costumes, shiny colours, a hook of a bassline, whistling lolly pops… Just groovy!

Pop Will Eat Itself
- 92 Degrees (Boilerhouse the Birth Mix)   *

If we called the '90s a melting pot, in which new crossbreeds of music genres ensued, then PWEI were the trailblazers of curious alchemy. They called their unpredictable alloy of danceable keys, guitar riffs, beats, and rapid mouthing 'intergalactic punk rock hip-hop'. It is resistant to stain and boredom.

Ice Cube - Who's the Mack   ×

It might seem shocking but hip-hop was here before mobile phones. It used to grow in the cracks of the rough suburban* city asphalt streets; it wasn't an artifice hydroponically grown under the lights of million-dollar business. It was not a made-to-measure product that follows the latest research, but an authentic statement of who is a hit and who is full of shit.

The Sundays - Here's Where the Story Ends   *

No matter how big or strong a person is, everybody is at some point, assaulted by fatigue from the daily fight with life. They then need to be encouraged and told everything will be alright, so they are able to go in for another round. The bare beauty of this song makes me want to hug the whole world, and even smile at the ticket inspector on the bus.

Alice in Chains - We Die Young   *

The first song from their debut album. An indication of the sound that took over the music charts within the next few months. A unique vocal style (many times imitated, but never surpassed), typical harmonized vocals. The cynical slogan 'We Die Young' was fiercely visionary – two of them are no longer with us.

Nirvana

Pearl Jam

Jesus Jones

Red Hot Chili Peppers

Ice-T

Primal Scream

Carter the Unstoppable Sex Machine

R.E.M.

2Pac

Massive Attack

Levellers

Metallica

Primus

U2

My Bloody Valentine

1991

A brief glance at the annual 1991 music statistics gives no indication that this year would be exceptional in any way. Even less so that it would be a breakthrough year and would significantly mark the face of popular music for the next few years. According to the Billboard 200 chart, which publishes the two hundred best-selling songs in the US weekly, the top spots were enjoyed longest by *Mariah Carey*, *Vanilla Ice*, and *Garth Brooks*, while the longest-running winners in the UK charts went to *Eurythmics*, *Cher*, and *Queen*. Look at the leading ranks of total sales at the end of the year, *Natalie Cole* and *Michael Bolton* could be added to the list, as well as *Simply Red* and *Tina Turner*. Had *Michael Jackson* released his multi-platinum new album *Dangerous* just a few weeks earlier than the end of November, he might have beaten them all. In other words, artisan pop was still en vogue. Looking more closely at the charts, one would also come across such names as *N.W.A.*, *Jesus Jones*, *R.E.M.*, or *Metallica*. Even though, in the context of the usual music bestsellers of the time, they seemed surprising, even out of place, they were a precursor of the upcoming big changes.

Aside from the mainstream, highly popular, rappers, hip-hop continued to push its boundaries and explore creative possibilities. *MC Hammer* and *Vanilla Ice* may have sold millions of records, but memorable albums that made history were released by others.

In 1991, *Ice-T* showed the harsh reality of life in a housing project on the outskirts of a big city on his fourth album *O.G.: Original Gangster*, creating one of the classic records of gangsta rap. *N.W.A.* also lived up to their gangster reputation when they brought another dark batch of songs full of street filth and violence on their album *Niggaz4Life*. The album became an unexpected hit and went platinum within two weeks of its release. *2Pac* also released his first solo album, fiercely criticising racism, police violence, and corruption. His *2Pacalypse Now* can be undoubtedly included in the treasure trove of US West Coast hip-hop.

However, the event that was to ultimately change the musical direction of the entire hip-hop scene in 1991 was not the release of a revolutionary record, but a precedent-setting court decision. In the case in question, the Irish singer *Gilbert O'Sullivan* successfully sued *Biz Markie* for the unauthorised use of a sample from one of his songs in the rapper's new single. As a result of this verdict, all samples used in henceforth new compositions must be cleared with their authors before the record is released. For hip-hop, this meant the end of one creative period. Many an album, essential to this genre, was created by masterfully combining literally dozens of samples, often within a single song. They could not be created nowadays, as sampling has become an extremely expensive working tool, only available to very rich or very brave artists.

The proponents of various forms of alternative rock were also more and more vocal, and the sound of their guitars was soon to dominate radio waves worldwide.

One of the flagships of the upcoming changes was *R.E.M.*, the epitome of a success story of an indie band that rose through hard work and relentless touring. They successfully entered the world of big music industry in 1988 with the record *Green*. After six albums in a span of six years and constant live performances, they took a time-out while preparing the follow-up (to *Green*). *Out of Time* was a triumphant return and the band won several music and platinum awards around the world. Even though it is hard to talk about their best or most cohesive work, the first single from this album, the timeless song *Losing My Religion*, became immortal. To this day, it is among not only the unforgettable moments of *R.E.M.*'s catalogue, but also of the entire '90s. *Dinosaur Jr.* also became veterans of the indie scene under the wings of a large distributor. The photo on the cover of their fourth album *Green Mind* catches one's eye, and although they had reduced the ear-shattering volume ever so slightly, the typical howling solos carried for over half the song are, unmistakably, proof that they were still roaring live with the same intensity. In 1991, *Smashing Pumpkins* were still fine-tuning the right balance between heavy rock riffs, lush psychedelic compositions and pop melodies. Their first album *Gish* had not made a big dent in the world just yet, but it already contained all the hallmarks that later made them into one of the most successful rock bands of their era.

After a long period of fascination with the synthetic sound of keyboards that defined the sound of the '80s, the guitar was a leading instrument once again and with it came the good old (not only rock, but also metal) riffs.

At the end of the 80s, glam metal was one of the most commercially successful music genres, with bands like *Mötley Crüe*, *Poison*, or *Cinderella* selling millions of records. Their popularity was also heavily supported by MTV, video clips of bands with stylised hairdos and flawless make-up formed a significant part of their daily menu. Nonetheless, fans of harder metal offshoots, for whom the night-time programme 'Headbangers Ball' was intended, did not go unnoticed. Every week, it brought them a fresh batch of video clips from the top metal scene as well as the deep underground for, at the time of its greatest popularity, up to an enormous length of three hours. There were studio interviews, but the show's team did not hesitate to travel and interview the bands during tours. American viewers most likely best remember the talkative presenter Riki Rachtman. He particularly liked the melodic genres of metal and, while out reporting about the bands, willingly participated in various adrenaline attractions, such as skydiving with *Megadeth* or visiting a water park with *Alice in Chains*. The Metalheads of Europe could take bets on what hair colour the host of the show Vanessa Warwick would have that week. Compared to her American colleague, her presenting style was more moderate, but her taste in music and the videos she played were all the more extreme.

Regardless their origin or preferences, both presenters would agree that *Metallica* took care of, for metal fans, the greatest and most discussed event of the year with their eponymous album. They took a risk on the novelty and pushed the frenzied tempos and epic, structured compositions, which were their hallmark, to the side-lines. With their more accessible sound, yet still honest metal material, and personal lyrics, the band conquered the world literally overnight. Orthodox fans may have gnashed their teeth, but, with their 'black album', Metallica built a gateway to the genre for millions of new supporters. For many, it destroyed the prejudices that metal is just a celebration of mindless revelry and cannot be played without eyeliner.

If there is a relationship between music and the latitude where it was created, it is no wonder that sunny Los Angeles became the centre of the entertainment-oriented glam metal scene. It also makes it easier to understand the nature of works of art by bands from rainy Seattle, located more than a thousand miles northwards.

The local scene was characterized by a dirty guitar sound, mixing early 70s heavy metal with punk influences, and energetic live shows. This mixture of down-tunes riffs as thick as mud, but delivered with soulful commitment, was labelled 'grunge' by music journalists. By strictly rejecting stage props, wearing ordinary worn-out clothes, and especially by the social and personal themes in their lyrics, grunge bands formed an almost perfect antithesis to stylised glam metal. After years of a quiet life on the fringes of the music scene, 1991 brought considerable media attention, including MTV, to the Seattle scene.

The programme 'Headbangers Ball' especially liked the charismatic *Alice in Chains*. After their video for *Man in the Box* took off there, MTV included it in daily rotation. Even though their debut *Facelift* had been released the year before, it suddenly sold like hot cakes and sales eventually reached a million. Thanks to that, they became the first in a line of grunge bands to go platinum and, at the same time, helped their followers tread their way onto daytime television screens. *Pearl Jam* also stopped by to present their first album on Headbangers Ball. Their singer Eddie Vedder used the presence of television cameras to spread music awareness and laid the groundwork for tweeting when he scribbled the name of his favourite band *Fugazi* on his arm during an interview. *Nirvana* did not avoid an invitation to the metal ball either, although the lead single *Smells Like Teen Spirit* from their new record *Nevermind* had its world premiere on another MTV program, 120 Minutes. Their frontman Kurt Cobain followed the prom etiquette in his own way and arrived at the studio in an extravagant dress.

Smells Like Teen Spirit became an unexpected hit shortly after its release. The song caught on both rock and student radio stations, and after a positive response to its video on its night-time schedule, MTV also started playing it during the day. For the next few weeks, it settled in the 'Buzz Bin' section – a menu of clips predicted to be a success on MTV, played several times a day.

Nirvana could be heard everywhere and *Nevermind*, its first effort for a major label, was beginning to make music history. The band recorded it with the intention of capturing a more intense pop sound.

Compared to their two-year-old independently released debut, on its follow-up, they played more with the dynamics of the songs and worked on the melodies, trying to break out of the sound template of the home grunge scene. And it succeeded, creating a captivating straightforward record filled with catchy songs. At that point, it had no idea it would start an avalanche of events to impact the world music scene. *Pearl Jam* debuted just a month earlier. Their album *Ten* was no sensation at first. They had only been playing together for a short time and had no audience, but they immediately went on tour to support the record. It lasted nine months, had 148 stops, and by its end, legends were already spreading about the band. The ferocious anthemic songs, the emotive, skin-piercing vocals, but especially the unbridled concerts caused fans to flock to stores to buy *Ten* even two years after its release. A new album was also recorded by the veterans of the grunge scene, *Soundgarden*. On *Badmotorfinger*, they considerably pushed the limits of their compositional mastery in a perfect mix of crushing riffs and vocal escapades, completing the year's batch of essential albums from Seattle, which documented the local musical diversity.

Nirvana's sound was nourished by the wildness of punk, *Pearl Jam* developed a hard rock legacy, and the complex work of *Soundgarden* unmistakably referenced metal. Therefore, although they were shaped by a similar environment and were labelled as the main representatives of grunge, with the growing artistic originality of their recordings, this designation was losing its justification.

Local music label Sub Pop played an important role in shaping the specific sound as well as the strong community spirit of the Seattle scene. It was formally founded in 1986 by Bruce Pavitt, loosely following on from his former music fanzine called 'Subterranean Pop'. However, the label was officially established two years later, when the promoter and music enthusiast with a business spirit Jonathan Poneman became a shareholder.

Among the first notable local bands in their catalogue to define the term grunge were *Soundgarden, Mudhoney,* and *TAD.* Their sound was produced by the engineer Jack Endino and his signature can be heard on most records from the early Sub Pop period. The album covers and promotional materials of the label stood out thanks to Charles Peterson's spontaneous black and white photos. They uniquely captured the energy-filled concerts and passionate fans, two key values of the label. For the devoted fans, or "losers", as they were affectionately called in the promo flyer, Pavitt and Poneman invented the popular 'Sub Pop Singles Club'. As part of it, they released for subscribers a limited edition 7" (vinyl record) every month; *Nirvana* having started the edition with their very first single. In the course of the years to come, such bands as *Afghan Whigs, L7, Fluid,* and many others contributed to it. *Nirvana* and *TAD* proved on a joint European tour in 1989 that grunge was not just a provincial attraction. They ended the tour in London, where they were joined by *Mudhoney,* and the influential British music press honoured them with enthusiastic reviews. The story of this legendary tour, which put Seattle on the map of world music, was later described by Bruce Pavitt in his book *Experiencing Nirvana: Grunge in Europe,* 1989 (2012).

The explosive popularity of grunge in 1991 made Sub Pop a globally respected brand. They continued to unearth great music, even though the 'grunge' label was rather a burden. They were just as happy to release the punk of *Supersuckers* or the folk rock of *The Walkabouts*; slow-core pioneers *Codeine* and *Mark Lanegan*'s acoustic ballads also found their home with them. Despite crises and weaker periods, Sub Pop is still in business to this day and lives up to its slogan: "We're not the best, but we're pretty good."

The 1990s, more than any other phase, made history as a period of prolific crossing of various, often seemingly incompatible, music genres. Even during the decades before, numerous experiments with different proportions of ingredients were conducted simultaneously on both sides of the Atlantic. However, it was not until the arrival of a new climate, favourable to alternative music forms, that multi-genre line-ups began to attract more attention.

On American soil, 1991 was a breakthrough year for several of them. In their eccentric work, *Fishbone* mixed funk, punk, ska, rock, and soul. They had been wowing concertgoers with this incredible mix since the early '80s, but it was not until *The Reality of My Surroundings* that they convinced both music critics and the general public about their qualities. Accidental contact with *Primus* could cause a mild shock to the uninitiated listener, as the surreal battle of virtuoso, funk-soaked bass riffs, and expressive metal guitar licks does not exactly sound like a recipe for commercial success. Nevertheless, the band won their first gold record for *Sailing the Seas of Cheese*, selling half a million copies in the US alone. Still, it was *Red Hot Chili Peppers* who shone brightest that year. After four albums and years of roaming the stages with their exotic hybrid of funk, rock, and rap vocals, the world finally fell under their spell during their fifth act; *Blood, Sugar, Sex, Magik*. From a cult club band, they unexpectedly became stars of international magnitude in the months to come.

Perry Farrel also bet on genre diversity when compiling the list of performers for the first year of his Lollapalooza travelling festival. Apart from his native *Jane's Addiction*, such different bands as *Siouxsie & The Banshees*, *Living Colour*, *Nine Inch Nails*, and *Butthole Surfers* took turns on one stage, and the success of the festival confirmed that the "alternative nation" welcomed the intermingling of musical genres with open arms.

In the meantime, intense testing of the limits of mutual compatibility between rock and electronic music carried on in Great Britain. Even though the Madchester scene pulled out all the trump cards the year before and had, thus, nothing new left to offer, its legacy caught on successfully. The British music press, therefore, quickly found new favourites and gave space to a wave of other, so-called alternative dance bands that developed it.

One of its leading representatives, *Jesus Jones*, made its mark with the album *Doubt*, on which they managed to mix the sound of guitars and dance beats, refreshed with samples, into an organic and melodically irresistible whole. They were particularly warmly received overseas, where their song *Right Here, Right Now* took over and fans snapped up tickets for their US tour before they even got on the plane. *EMF* used a similar dough to bake their debut *Schubert Dip* and started their career at light speed. With their first single *Unbelievable*, they hit the charts all over Europe and even climbed to the top of the American singles chart. However, just as both bands rode on a similarly successful wave, their subsequent fate was also alike when, despite the effort to develop their artistic expression, they failed to make a significant impression with their follow-up records. *Primal Scream* took a completely different approach when creating their new sound. They originally started as an indie pop band with jangling guitars but, later on, switched to noisier garage rock. After the success of the dance remix of one of their older songs, they decided to record a whole new record in a similar spirit. The author of the remix, the DJ Andrew Weatherall, also helped them with the production during its recording. The resulting innovation exceeded all expectations, a colourful collage of beats, live instruments, samples, and vocals erased the boundaries between remix and traditional song form. The *Screamadelica* album became a genre milestone, which is still a respected example of the fusion of dance music and rock'n'roll.

It was not only dance rhythms that echoed on the British Isles in 1991. A lot of guitar music was also born although, paradoxically, one of the greatest rock records of the year owed its uniqueness to modern production methods and the influence of electronic music.

U2 almost broke up during the recording but the *Achtung Baby* album ended up being their strongest collection of songs to date. On it, they managed to redefine their sound, absorb new inspiration and, at the same time, maintain their own identity. *My Bloody Valentine* spent two years trying the nerves of their publisher and the patience of the technicians from nineteen different recording studios until they were finally happy with the sound of their new release. The long wait was worth it, the disjointed guitar walls from *Loveless* are still remembered 30 years later as a sonic adventure and mandatory study material for bands from the 'shoegaze' scene.

The musical visions of *Ned's Atomic Dustbin* drew from a completely different barrel. Instead of following technological trends or experimenting with studio equipment, they opted to add a second bass guitarist to the line-up, vis-a-vis achieving a completely unique sound. With an extra dose of enthusiasm and catchy melodies, they immortalised it on their debut *God Fodder*. At home, they earned a reputation of a club magnet thanks to their wild concerts, and their videos were often played overseas on MTV's 120 Minutes. *Teenage Fanclub* did not lack a large overseas fan club either. Their songs, combining typical British melodics with half an ear for the sound of American-style alternative rock did very well in the local singles chart. Still, the band was paid the greatest tribute by the editorial of the *SPIN* magazine, calling *Bandwagonesque*, in the annual poll, the album of the year. Although history has proved other versions of the rankings to be true, the record has lost none of its quality even after all those years.

Those who were not fans of mainstream pop music in the average British household were not limited to cable TV. BBC2, a national TV channel, aired a twice-weekly half-hour block called 'SNUB TV', a boon to all fans of alternative music.

Apart from playing videos, the programme also focused on recordings of concert performances and interviews with bands that were currently stirring the waters of not only the domestic but also the American independent scene. It not only followed the hot trail of Madchester, post-punk, shoegaze, indie pop, and alternative rock, but it was not against detours to hip-hop, industrial, or early experiments with electronic music. There was no presenter to be seen in the broadcast; instead, the performers spoke directly to the camera during the interviews, which greatly increased the sense of authenticity. SNUB TV supplied fans with music news for three years, with 1991 being the last year, at least leaving behind the second of a pair of VHS selections featuring the best of the broadcast live performances of such bands as *Happy Mondays*, *The Fall*, *Ride*, *The House of Love*, and *Pixies*.

However, that was not the only deserving deed in the field of home video that year. Creation Records made fans of dream pop and the nascent shoegaze scene, drenched in layers of distorted guitar sound, happy by continuing their video compilation with clips by *Slowdive*, *The Telescopes* or *Swervedriver*. *Sub Pop Video Network Program 1* contains a lot of hair, sweat, and especially loud and dirty rock'n'roll in the form of early visual attempts not only by the well-known trio of bands that introduced Europe to the Sub Pop brand some time before. *Video Sampler 1* by *Wax Trax!* is also worth mentioning, as it provided an uncompromising confrontation with the work of the industrial sound terrorists *Front Line Assembly*, *Young Gods*, *Front 242*, and others.

The rise in popularity of alternative music genres and their gradual penetration into the mainstream was also reflected in the list of performers as well as nominees in individual genre categories at the 1991 MTV Video Music Awards.

The most (more specifically, ten) nominations were earned by *R.E.M.* for the video to their *Losing My Religion*. Michael Stipe, the lead singer of the band, had prepared a set of different colour T-shirts for the occasion; on each of them, with an apt slogan, he expressed his support for issues ranging from racial equality and safe sex to the right to vote and the regulation of the possession of firearms. He intended to come and collect each of the potential awards in a different one of them. Ultimately, his original campaign was successful, as *R.E.M.* was pulled out of the envelope as many as six times, once for the Video of the Year.

Jesus Jones were the only representatives of the UK's export music to win an award; for Best New Artist Video. Their compatriots *EMF*, on the other hand, got the chance to bring the current sound of the island's alternative dance scene to the audience live via satellite transmission from a London club. Their performance did not lack the appropriate energy and drive, although a few tips in the area of dress sense would definitely go a long way. By contrast, *Metallica* invaded the stage without any visual masquerade. A belligerently crouched James Hetfield sang with determination and the rest of the band did not lag behind him in the slightest. Anyone trying to keep up with Jason Newsted's headbanging without years of training might as well get ready to see a chiropractor the next day. They gave an honest concert rather than showy TV entertainment, the nature of their performance, thus, symbolically foreshadowing the direction in which musical values and visual aesthetics would go in the following years.

Not only was *EMF*'s hit *Unbelievable* performed live, but the accompanying music video was also up for Best Dance Video, marking the start of Josh Taft's directing career in the music industry.

He continued his work almost until the end of the '90s and made a significant mark in the consciousness of music video fans with several of his over two dozen works. He enjoyed working with captivating black and white imagery and liked to use atypical framing of shots. As a Seattle native, he was close to the local music scene, which is why it is no surprise he had a hand in music videos for *Mother Love Bone*, *Mad Season*, *Brad*, and *Pearl Jam*. Eddie Vedder's disgruntled complaint about the lights in the hall during the opening of their *Even Flow* video was directed at him. He also co-directed the music video for the song *Would?*, *Alice in Chains'* top number and one of the most famous grunge songs ever. However, he did not only work for bands from his hometown; he also cooperated with such bands as *Midnight Oil, Manic Street Preachers, Meat Puppets,* and *Stone Temple Pilots.* In 1993, the latter band took home an astronaut statuette from the MTV Video Music Awards for Best Video by a New Artist for the song *Plush,* which was his doings. Although he did most of his work for rock artists, he also had a weak spot for hip-hop, as evidenced by *Cypress Hill, Nas,* or *A Tribe Called Quest,* for whom he recorded a few successful pieces.

During the late '90s, Josh Taft changed his focus, becoming a sought-after and multi-awarded creator of commercials for such companies as Nike, Adidas, Coca-Cola, Nissan, and many others. Most recently, he ventured into documentary for a change, when he presented at the Seattle International Film Festival his film *Alive & Well* (2013) focusing on the stories of people suffering from Huntington's disease. It is not clear whether he is still planning to return to making video clips at some point. Let us hope the time comes when he hears the calling again.

The following pages feature video clips shot in support of singles released in 1991.

Selected and commented on by:
~ Shezz, + Zebra, # Aran, * Rasťo, ‡ Veni, × Kubsson,

Galactic Cowboys - I'm Not Amused *

An intro from a Mexican bullfighting arena? OK. Metal riffs for headbanging? I'm fine with that. Beatlesque three-part harmonies? I like. A mouth organ solo? Refreshing. But pack it all into one song? Not many people 'got' Galactic Cowboys, but a bunch of dedicated ones will always stick up for this underrated band. I'm one of those people.

Red Hot Chili Peppers - Suck My Kiss ~

A great song about oral sex, with a video focusing on forces returning home from the Gulf? I don't get it either! But with such punchy bass and drums, and slick guitar riffs, who cares. But we have to remember, this was made when they were more experimental, and not as focused on selling records like now.

Tar - Goethe

Tar – Jackson. The best 'Noise' album of all time. Better than everything that The Jesus Lizard, Killdozer, Shellac, Big Black, or Cows ever done put together. Ultimate, genre defining, epochal. The best ROCK record in history.

My Bloody Valentine - Soon   +

Walls of sound coming out of the fuzzy guitar in the hands of a bloke who stares at his own shoes all the time. The golden age of shoegaze. The carefree pairing of a violin loop with nearly danceable rhythms. Can you hear it there? You would do better to watch the video! The music and the video are two sides of the same coin in this case.

Spin Doctors - Two Princes   ~

Not a one hit wonder, but pretty close. It shouldn't work, but it somehow does. With lyrics that would make Shakespeare sleep easy at night and with musicians that Zeppelin would not fear, this band managed to smash out their belter with ease. So catchy, so simple, so bad that it's good. A lesson, be good at being bad.

Saint Etienne - Nothing Can Stop Us   *

Saint Etienne stirred the waters of the indie dance scene by using a unique combination of current dance rhythms with arrangements and pop sounds three decades older. Slightly romantic and naive, contagiously playful, and melodic, and when they came across the charming singer Sarah Cracknell, they knew that nothing could stop them.

Pearl Jam - Oceans ~

Pearl Jam do not make many music videos, but when they do, they make them just perfect. An inspiring surfer I was not, until watching this, now a keen amateur. Great example of Eddie's captivating and haunting vocals with an orchestral feel, using a tympani and even a fire extinguisher to enhance the sound.

Ned's Atomic Dustbin - Grey Cell Green

It was not possible to overlook this band in the crowd of English guitar bands of the first half of the '90s. No psychedelic dance songs, no Rolling Stones quotations. Instead, rousing, energetic garage music with contagious positive energy. On top of that, Ned's had two basses, so I listened to them also as a matter of study.

The Smashing Pumpkins - Siva +

The song 'Siva' is based on Hendrix's chord (7#9). It started to write the history of one of the most original bands of the '90s. Perfectionist song structures and the unmistakable sound of this band has an astounding power even two decades on. SP had a 'logo' in the shape of a heart – they struck mine perfectly, and forever.

Lenny Kravitz - Always on the Run   +

If Slash pens a guitar riff for somebody else, nothing but a real rock'n'roll smash can be created. If that somebody else is Lenny Kravitz, he develops the given motif into perfection whilst citing existential life advice from his mother. But a rocker is only a rocker if he follows his own path. In this case, it is an escape to look for your own truth.

Primus - Jerry Was a Race Car Driver   *

In the brief magical period that the first half or the '90s was, even a weird band was allowed to be signed to a major label. Just like this head-on collision between musical virtuosity and cartoon grotesque singing. When watching this video, it is hard to believe your own eyes and ears. Still, the only sane solution is to play it again.

Temple of the Dog - Hunger Strike   ~

This song is simply the best 'duet' ever. Vedder and Cornell became living* legends to many of the fans from the genre, and easy to see why. Stunning vocals and guitar riffs, beautiful lyrics, simply perfection, and with Eddie and Chris together, you get the perfect threesome, says my girlfriend!

Dinosaur Jr. - The Wagon

The greatest hit by Dinosaur Jr.? Many people would say 'Freak Scene'. Yoz loves 'Feel the Pain'. For me, it will forever be this amazing song, which seems to have finished before it's supposed to and which, to a large extent, defines my '90s in Prague. Melancholy wrapped in beautiful guitar mess. PURE MASTERPIECE.

2Pac - If My Homie Calls +

Tupac Amaru Shakur. A Ghetto boy. The best forever. The Fairy Godmother gave him the gift of a huge talent. He had several names and faces. In spite of an early violent death, he had a taste of fame, was appreciated and became a legend of the hip-hop scene. However, he never forgot where he came from and who his true homies were. It is they who this song is dedicated to.

Ugly Kid Joe - Everything About You +

Not even a poor budget for the video discouraged the larky director from spending it on erotic blow-up dolls and a large tank of helium to fill them up with. Problems only started when a few of them flew away. So Ugly Kid Joe had to face complaints of the pilots from a nearby airport, saying that in their flight paths, were some very busty kites floating around.

EMF - I Believe *

Too much of anything can be harmful, even luck. 'Epsom Mad Funkers' had a load of it when they broke through with their first 'Unbelievable' single. Their sound was dominated by fat dance beats improved with the right measure of rock energy and pop melodies. But although thez believed they were capable of delivering, they never repeated their primary success.

Massive Attack - Unfinished Sympathy ~

First, I do not like this type of music. Second, this song is simply amazing. Confusing and conflicting statements remind me of it. It should not work, but it just does. Technically brilliant with loops of different speeds, it almost sounds out of sync, but in a fantastic way. A symphony of sounds combine.

Siouxsie and the Banshees - Kiss Them For Me

I've always liked Siouxsie. There is a kind of eerie 'femininity' about her. Not a girlie girl, but an experienced lady with a beautiful voice. With 'Superstition' this band had already peaked, but actually, this single is beautiful. One of the few songs of 'Western' pop music where the oriental motive does not sound stupid or cheap.

Nirvana - In Bloom *

I first listened to 'Nevermind' on a hissing tape. It travelled from hand to hand, and it had the name of the band carelessly scribbled on it. I had not heard of Nirvana, I had not seen a single picture or a video. There was no need. When the tape finished, I knew all I needed to know, fundamentally marked by the power of their music alone.

Red Hot Chili Peppers - Give It Away *

At the time when they didn't have to have their "typical radio-friendly chorus" in each song, they were able to be really as hot as chili and provoke wild actions. I was always too shy to dance; I thought I couldn't do that. But after a lesson from these four asylum patients, I suddenly got it. All you need is to forget that people are watching, and pretty much anything can pass as dancing.

The Bats - The Black And The Blue *

Maybe even more difficult than to come up with something ground-breakingly original is to be superior in a field that has been ploughed a thousand times before. You won't find many cases in which guitar pop sounds this fresh and zealous. Perfectly harmonised vocals, unworn melodies and the beautiful jangly guitars of The Bats are therefore an unexpected delight. A New Zealand Pavlova with kiwifruit for your ears.

Levellers - One Way ~

A Brighton pub band done good. I lived and played there, but without success. These guys showed that a "pub-folk" style can make it into the charts whilst staying true to their musical roots by the use of many folk instruments. You can't help but feel the 'hook' in every song and this is certainly no different.

Noir Désir - En route pour la joie

An awesome band with a sad destiny. Besides their amazing and fierce songs with "Dischord energy", I have always admired Noir Désir for their ability to work French into rock beautifully. And I was also lucky enough to see them live, sometime in 1991 during their gig alongside Vladimír Mišík (sic!).

Cypress Hill - Phuncky Feel One +

When hip-hop was still in nappies*, it used to fill them mostly with treasures. Ones like Cypress Hill. They have solid 'phuncky' beats soaked in psychedelic anaesthetic from Mexican tequila. They also have a frontman B-Real, whose nasal rapping style would not be destroyed even by using nose drops 'Muconasal Plus' with hyaluronic acid!

Pearl Jam - Alive   *

Prague, September 22nd, 2006. An excited crowd returning from a Pearl Jam gig taking the subway carriage home. In the euphoric atmosphere, a Polish fan climbed up the handrails and started to sing. Gradually, more of them joined in and, in the next moment, a mighty chant of dozens of throats was sweeping through the train. We sang 'Alive'. And every single one of us felt that way.

American Music Club - Rise   *

Things are not always what they seem. The first impression might be misleading, and you find out that the reality is different from what you expected. This anthemic single enticed me into the troubled, poetic, and intimate world of Mark Eitzel, in which no other song sounds like 'Rise'. But I do not feel cheated. I got much more than I had hoped for.

Carter USM - Bloodsport for All   ~

A 13-year old boy, searching for his generation's version of 'Sex Pistols', this boy found Carter USM, and a happy man I have been since. Underrated and never overplayed, they sung and played songs that filled me with every possible emotion. Although not the most known song by them, this is still a gem.

Anthrax - Bring The Noise (ft. Public Enemy)

This song has grown old over the years. But those who say they do not do headbanging to its rhythm anymore are talking crap. It is genre defining and still fun. There is a great comment on YouTube under this video: "It is sad that the guitarist from the metal band rapped better twenty years ago than lots of famous rappers today".

Soundgarden - Rusty Cage +

A wah-wah pedal that's so damn low. A guitar riff with the sound of flaking rust. A stirring tempo accompanied by earnest vocals full of messages about internal freedom from all that imprisons us. Although we have broken teeth and bruised knuckles, let's never surrender. Every cage gets rusty one day. All that is left is a free run.

Jesus Jones - Right Here, Right Now ~

Their biggest hit and most well-known song, in fact, most people can name the song, but not the band. I'm not a believer in many things, but I do believe in 'Jesus Jones' and the message they spread. I just love the coarse tone and then high pitch changes in his voice, and of course that typical indie beat.

Fishbone - Sunless Saturday   *

A dose of energy for when the days don't click and I need a kick start. When listening to this, I jump as if the floor was plugged into high voltage. Great intro, great riff, great chorus. If I had to face a professional boxer in the ring, I'd have this on before the bout. He would probably kill me, but I would deliver one serious punch too.

R.E.M. - Radio Song   ~

One of the more controversial songs by REM, which split the fans. Those who did not like the rap and the fact it has a very similar melody to 'Night Swimming', and those who just appreciated everything this great band had done. I was in the latter group. With the band now split up, any song by them is a classic.

Throwing Muses - Counting Backwards   *

I like bands in which the women not only sing but also play. They bring into the music another dimension, a different feel, and whole other dynamics. Two beautiful and talented ones met in Throwing Muses and the then exclusively English label '4AD' signed them as their first American band. National pride must be left aside when such a unique phenomenon is the case!

N.W.A. - Appetite For Destruction   +

A city of crime. Young lives full of violence. Breathtaking stories from the streets. The city of Compton, LA, California. The early nineties. Words and bullets only weigh heavy when it's real. Splinters of everyday reality stuck deep in the soul. Pumping beats, a machine gun flow and an unchained appetite for destruction. Talented gangsters N.W.A.

U2 - Mysterious Ways   ‡

A video shining with colours, not quite fitting in with the nature of their work. However, the belly dancer fits in, the one the singer has dreamed up and the guitar player later married. The guitar sound is as full and enriching as usual, holding up to the tradition of 'British Isles rock'. But what rock has in common with the Arabic world, only Bono probably knows.

Beat Happening - Hot Chocolate Boy   *

Seems like anyone could have composed this. Like, why did they leave out the bass? And did the singer really have to be so sloppy? But their enthusiasm was honest, their naivety charming, and their songs incredibly catchy. Listening to their album is like looking at pictures drawn by your little brother – you wouldn't judge him. And what is more, you will never draw any like those.

EMF - Unbelieveable ~

Every compilation tape or CD ever released seems to have this on, as it crosses so many genres whilst belonging to none. It is surprising then that this contains profanity which is never edited out, but still gets so much airtime. Listen to the chorus again, in the background, how've you missed it, unbelievable.

Pixies - Alec Eiffel *

Although Pixies were one of the most influential indie rock bands at the beginning of the MTV boom, it did not hit them. They were known for their aversion to shooting music videos. But playing in a wind-tunnel? Who could resist! 'Trompe le Monde' was their swan song; however, they still had a couple of aces up their sleeves, as 'Alec Eiffel' proves.

Mercury Rev - Car Wash Hair +

This song was a single even before their debut album "Yerself Is Steam" was released, and it appeared as a hidden track – number 99. It has a modest, simple, melody, to which layers of guitars, horns, and percussion are building in sequence. With slightly naive and equivocal lyrics of the song, it just exaggerates the overall playful mood.

Nirvana - Smells Like Teen Spirit ~

I could choose to be a 'grunger' or to be a 'raver'. I enjoyed both kinds of music, but when I heard this, my mind was made up. So, the hair grew long, the drums and guitar got learned, and the life-long passion of this music started. Simply the anthem of my teens, a generation, and forever the ultimate riff.

Primal Scream - Come Together *

Whoever expected correctly that, in 1990, Primal Scream would have the potential to record a revolutionary album, surely must have owned a working crystal ball. Formerly retro rockers, with not much of a personality, turned out to be sound visionaries who pulled down the boundaries between the club dance scene and the mainstream. This creative scream of theirs is inspirational to this day.

Blur - She's So High ~

Blur vs Oasis, close your eyes and listen for 20 seconds, which band is it? Blur were clever as they changed and adapted their music to suit those who were not Beatles fans, sorry, Oasis fans! This, their debut track, is still a fan favourite and also one of their most played live songs. Simple but effective.

Davová psychóza - Mozgová paralýza *

This piece from the prehistoric times of Slovak music video art, perhaps evokes a smile nowadays. But wild gigs, an unmistakable sound, Jano's typical phrasing and fervent lyrics critical of society, have made everlasting legends out of 'Davovka'. The first punk vinyl I ever bought, and the last one I'd want to get rid of.

MC 900 Ft. Jesus - Killer Inside Me *

The ninth decade of the 20th century brought a few surprising findings. Some white men can jump, some music genres are destined to break out of the underground into the spotlights and some white men can even rap. Here is an early attempt to prove that a funky beat and smartly used scratching have a future. 900 % success.

Metallica - Enter Sandman ×

Four angry men. With their hypnotising bass lines, a hammer and anvil of two guitars, rushed by a whipping rhythm, they spoke to legions of their devotees. Together, they turned a blind eye to the mainstream. But here, they reduced their anger a bit and added a riff which dazed everyone. They are suddenly so big that they can be classed as mainstream themselves. So f***ing what?

Kitchens of Distinction - Drive That Fast   *

Perhaps, we all subconsciously look for the feeling of happiness. The thorny road to it is bordered by attempts, mistakes, and disappointments, while happiness is usually so fragile and elusive. Maybe that is why the majority of the most beautiful works of human art are inspired by a range of feelings preceding to finding it, like this romantic confession about a possible 'might'.

Tři sestry - Zelená   ‡

Their music was created in a pub where most protagonists spent swathes of their time, their life materialised in unorthodox lyrics and performances in a theatrical style. There are people who can sing and play perfectly, but never find an audience. This Czech pub rock legend sounds far from perfect; yet, their fans have been devoted to them for 25 years.

R.E.M. - Losing My Religion   *

The best things I have experienced just happened to me. I did not speculate and instinctively took a ride on the wave of destiny. Therefore, I am not surprised how this song, which has not lost any of its urgency after 25 years neither, was created. The guitarist was learning how to play the mandolin and, while doing so, unintentionally wrote it! What are the chances you could plan something like that?

1992

Beastie Boys

Rage Against the Machine

Pantera

Stone Temple Pilots

Helmet

Ministry

Faith No More

The Jesus and Mary Chain

Stereo MC's

Blind Melon

James

The Prodigy

Soul Asylum

Manic Street Preachers

Ugly Kid Joe

WOULD?

(CANTRELL)
KNOW ME BROKEN BY MY MASTER
TEACH THEE ON CHILD OF LOVE HEREAFTER

INTO THE FLOOD AGAIN
SAME OLD TRIP IT WAS BACK THEN
SO I MADE A BIG MISTAKE
TRY TO SEE IT ONCE MY WAY

DRIFTING BODY ITS SOLE DESERTION
FLYING NOT YET QUITE THE NOTION

AM I WRONG?
HAVE I RUN TOO FAR TO GET HOME
HAVE I GONE
AND LEFT YOU HERE ALONE
IF I WOULD, COULD YOU?

1992

In 1991, the total number of units sold on the American music market recorded a year-on-year decrease. The artists established in the 1980s failed to meet the commercial expectations of their labels as well as appeal to music lovers from Generation X, now coming of age. They needed a cultural revolution just as their parents' generation needed it in the late '60s and '70s. In an attempt to make up for the missing turnovers, record companies turned their attention to, up to that point, marginal subcultures and genres, which had their own loyal audiences and, thus, a potential for purchasing power. Music journalists enthusiastically praised the new names and several promising titles saw the light of day, but they were still hoping for some 'big event' that would show the stagnant industry a new direction. That event turned out to be the release of *Nirvana*'s album *Nevermind*, having quickly climbed up the Billboard 200. Its path was marked by the single *Smells Like Teen Spirit*, which spread through the airwaves like wildfire, and its accompanying video drove crowds of young music fans into raptures. In the week ending January 11th, 1992, *Nevermind* dethroned the King of Pop, Michael Jackson, and his album *Dangerous* from the top of the album charts, symbolically heralding the arrival of a new musical era.

The unexpected commercial success of Nevermind ruffled the sleek feathers of the music mainstream. Out of the blue, there was a demand for noisy guitars, and the initially local sound of 'grunge' became a hot commodity within months. The magic marketing buzzword promising the sale of millions of records was quickly adopted by record company promotions and music journalists. The label 'grunge' was suddenly used for anything and everything, often to the surprise of the very bands that were labelled with it.

The major label debut by one of the original few to define the genre, Seattle's *Mudhoney*, was released in 1992. Although they had prepared their, to date, most diverse record and included their typical garage sound, paradoxically, neither critics nor fans, now affected by grunge fever, showed much enthusiasm for their *Piece of Cake*. L7, the founders of a series of benefit concert called Rock for Choice, enjoyed more attention. Not only at these concerts but also on their breakthrough album *Bricks Are Heavy*, seasoned with punk and metal, they drew attention to the interests and issues of the female part of the rock world. In this way, they secured their place among the most distinctive all-female bands of the '90s.

Alice in Chains skyrocketed to stardom, although the lyrics of their multi-platinum record *Dirt* mostly dealt with such heavy topics as depression or drug addiction. On it, the band's sound was considerably darker and musically harder, thanks to which it also gained respect among metal fans. On the day when their dark opus came out, *Stone Temple Pilots* from San Diego also released their debut album named *Core*. Fans received the record with enthusiasm, unlike critics who accused the band of plagiarism and feeding on the currently modern sound of Seattle. It took several years and albums before critics had mercy on them and recognised that their early work deserved to be in the grunge era hall of fame.

The grunge phenomenon caused an increased interest of major labels in other local subcultures of the musical underground. These were closely linked to the activities of independent labels. In the same way that Sub Pop was behind the creation of grunge and Amphetamine Reptile synonymous with 'noise rock', people went to Dischord Records to get some 'post-hardcore' and anyone looking for some wild and original rock music certainly did not go home empty-handed at Touch and Go.

Unexpected possibilities suddenly opened up for many of those bands who had previously operated in an environment of strict 'do-it-yourself' ethics. Talent scouts from record companies and their employers, lured by the idea of the musical underground as a gold mine, were willing to invest considerable resources in them. Some of the bands decided to risk losing credibility with their orthodox fans and look into the world of big business music.

As some behind-the-scenes rumours had it, *Helmet* received an incredible million dollar advance to switch to a new label. They rose to the challenge head on. On *Meantime*, they did not take a step away from their raw sound, creating an uncompromisingly hard record, rolling over anything in its path. Before long, *Jawbox* was also to lose their indie status, and anyone who heard their full-blooded album *Novelty*, released in 1992, must have known why. With this album, they ranked among the best that the post-hardcore scene had to offer. By contrast, anyone who had ever experienced a concert by *The Jesus Lizard*, or had faced the storm that they performed on their record *Liar*, probably had a hard time imagining that any label head would allow them into the office one day. Ultimately, none of the bands benefited significantly from cooperation with a big label. Artistically, they held their own, stayed true to themselves, and recorded some of their best work ever; however, they failed to reach a wider audience. It turned out that underground is underground for a reason – for mass taste, it is, simply, too… 'underground'.

The Touch and Go label is one of the unshakable pillars of the American indie rock scene. Its creation was preceded by an eponymous music fanzine, founded in 1979 by a teacher and punk, Tesco Vee. He started the label two years later with singles by some sympatico hardcore punk bands, and was, in the same year, joined by Corey Rusk, the bassist of one of them. Their cooperation ended in 1983 when Corey Rusk assumed responsibility for the label's future direction.

Touch and Go had already built a reputation as a respected independent brand in the '80s. Loud, aggressive, and disharmonious bands found a home under their roof but, at the same time, they pushed genre boundaries as well as a means of artistic expression in rock music. No contracts were signed with the bands, their mutual cooperation worked on the basis of a gentleman's agreement, according to which the net profit from the sales of the records were equally divided between the band and the label, for which the label reserved the right to reissue the record in case it sold out. Thanks to this, the label always had an almost complete catalogue on offer, which was a real rarity in the days before digital distribution.

In the 1990s, they broadened their scope by including less sonically intense ensembles. Apart from the flagship bands following their rumbling past, such as post-hardcore greats *The Jesus Lizard*, *Shellac*, or *Girls Against Boys*, the punk rockers of *Arcwelder* were also happy to settle here, while *Urge Overkill* paid tribute to orthodox rock'n'roll. The strong presence of keyboards did not take anything away from the wild temperament of *Brainiac*, while *Seam* scored even with the more sensitive listener thanks to rationing tension patiently and gradually. The sound diversity of the Touch and Go catalogue is underlined by *Polvo*'s guitar experiments, brought to anti-melodic perfection or, perhaps, by *Calexico*'s playful compositions that flirt with film music.

After more than a quarter of a century of operation, the unfavourable economic situation forced the label to limit their activities and stop releasing new music. Until they change their minds, we will have to make do with the more than four hundred great records they have released or reminisce about their very beginnings with the book entitled *Touch and Go: The Complete Hardcore Punk Zine '79-'83* (2010).

MTV Europe promptly responded to the hysteria that broke out around Nirvana and included 'Alternative Nation', a two-hour programme, in their scheduling. Every week, the rising stars of the wider alternative scene, as well as strange line-ups from the hidden corners of the musical underground, were shed light on by Toby Amies with dandily gelled hair.

It is often just a lucky coincidence that decides whether a band will captivate their audiences. Some bands, such as *Screaming Trees*, experienced it first-hand. They had released five albums, had had countless fistfights, and held a reputation as a cult band, when they recorded their album *Sweet Oblivion*. But it was not until their song *Nearly Lost You* was included on the soundtrack of the movie *Singles* (1992) that their psychedelic hard rock and Mark Lanegan's bewitching baritone opened the door to a larger number of fans. Promotion by means of a film also played an important role in the musical career of *The Lemonheads*. They attracted attention when they spiced up the famous *Mrs. Robinson* from *The Graduate* (1967) with a dash of punk to make it sound like their own. Only then did the listeners notice that the original songs from their new album *It's a Shame About Ray* are not to be sneezed at.

Soul Asylum had been building their live reputation since the early '80s. They had a punk energy and a bed-headed singer in ripped jeans with a properly tattered image, who seemed to have been cut out of a grunge encyclopaedia. But it was not until MTV aired their emotional video for the song *Runaway Train*, which helped find a number of lost children across the United States, that their current album *Grave Dancers Union* started selling at breakneck speed. In contrast, *Blind Melon* was a completely new band, although with their hippie look and undisguised love for '70s rock, they seemed to have been playing in bars for at least two decades. Their eponymous first album languished on the shelves without much response for almost a year, until they shot a light-hearted music video with an annoyingly cute dancing bee in the main role. The video for *No Rain* remains one of the most memorable shown on MTV during the '90s, and, within months, the band became a massively popular concert attraction.

Alternative rock and grunge very quickly found themselves in the centre of the action in the field of hard guitar music. Glam metal, central up until that point, suddenly found itself on the side-lines, but the decline in the popularity of bands with a stylised image in no way meant a decline in interest in metal music. Even those metalheads who did not strictly listen to extreme underground genres but, at the same time, wanted to shake their heads to something harder than the new *Def Leppard* album, had several reasons to be cheerful in 1992.

Fans of B-movies, horror, and cheap thrills could easily fall in love with *White Zombie*. After a series of independent recordings, they managed to earn the trust of a major label, which they did not disappoint with *La Sexorcisto: Devil Music Volume One*. A continuous stream of metal riffs interspersed with excerpts from obscure films gives the impression of an extravagant metal party in a godforsaken video rental store. Following the record, a great number of fans made it possible for them to go on a two-year tour and provided for generous support from MTV. *Pantera* went through a drastic genre change on their previous album while, on the next one, they confirmed that they stood behind their new musical direction one hundred and twenty percent. *Vulgar Display of Power* is a more than apt name for this collection of songs with a dense groove and coarse vocals, and the cowboys from hell had definitively erased the traces of their glam metal past.

Following the path that *Metallica* had indicated in the previous year, their traditional companions and rivals also joined the imaginary struggle for the thrash metal throne. *Megadeth* slowed down significantly, simplified their compositions towards greater songfulness, and, in contrast to the past, added strong melodies. This resulted in the most commercially successful album of their entire, long, career, one they do not have to be ashamed of even with the passing of time. Today, *Countdown to Extinction* can easily be included among the most essential metal records of the '90s.

Metal elements also proved to be excellent material for combining with other musical genres. Loud guitar riffs and pounding drums found particularly good use in the creation of 'industrial'. Industrial music had been around in various forms since the mid-1970s. Since its creation, it had carried elements of modern technologies, extreme sound processes and noise surfaces, created either by layering distorted electronic noises or by using percussion instruments of an industrial nature, i.e., the sounds of hammers, anvils, chains, and other implements. The influence of industrial processes can be found to varying degrees in several music genres, industrial metal particularly gaining popularity in the 1990s.

Among its most successful representatives were *Nine Inch Nails*. On the mini-album, *Broken*, they presented themselves with a raw sound, combining a distorted pulse of synthesizer loops with aggressive guitars and furious vocals. The band also created video clips for most of the songs; however, all but one were denied broadcast worldwide due to the extremeness of the images, which did not lag behind their musical side. On their fifth studio effort *Psalm 69*, *Ministry*, for a change, partially deviated from the sound of synthesizers and electronics and, instead, decided to confront the resistance of their audience's eardrums with an increased emphasis on metal riffs and frenetic tempos. England's *Godflesh* were a respected name on the European industrial scene. Massive walls of guitar noise, compositions pressured with an unsettling atmosphere, and a repetitive machine rhythm made the *Pure* album a truly neat example of a walk down a hostile production line.

The travelling multi-genre festival Lollapalooza promoted the prominence of industrial, with *Nine Inch Nails* and *Ministry* being among its headliners of the first two years. The sales of both bands' records from this period reached platinum in the following years.

Thanks to its wide range of genres, the Lollapalooza festival managed to bring together even such diametrically opposed music worlds as rock and hip-hop. Although it was alternative guitar bands that were the focus of its billing, representatives of the hip-hop scene were also featured on the diverse list of performers in the first year.

It was here that *Body Count*, a rock band with the rapper *Ice-T* behind the microphone, had their concert premiere. Despite the fact that he does not actually rap at all on this eponymous debut from 1992, this record is considered one of the milestones of rap-metal. Musically, they drew on heavy metal and punk rock, but the lyrics are firmly rooted in hip-hop culture, both in their themes and, especially, language. The lyrics of the album caused a big uproar at the time of its release, mainly due to its vulgarity, brutality, and ill-conceived irony. Inappropriate entertainment, dark humour, and, also, apt social criticism was a thorn in the side of many. Supporters of political correctness were appalled, and the band got into hot water even in the US Senate. To one's surprise, the revolutionaries from *Rage Against the Machine* had no problems connected to the contents of their lyrics. On their first, eponymous, album, they perfected the concept of rap-metal not only in terms of the content but also the form. They took an explosive mixture of metal riffs and hip-hop-influenced rhythms and combined it with venomous, left-wing rap into a single entity. A year later, they became the main headliner of Lollapalooza, having also performed on the side stage the year before.

Faith No More earned the label of a rap-metal band based on the huge success of a single called *Epic* from their previous record. On their new album *Angel Dust*, they boldly drank from the well of creativity and composed an experimental, sonic puzzle that left not only many music critics but also their listeners rather dizzy. The American audience received the record half-heartedly, but European listeners took to it much more kindly. Maybe that is why *Faith No More* never got invited to Lollapalooza. Still, thanks to this record they broke the rap-metal curse for good.

Even though hip-hop intermingled with other genres and, thus, gave rise to new offshoots, it did not stagnate in its pure form either. Its breeding ground was mainly two traditional localities, in which it had been growing and developing in parallel since its birth in the mid-1970s. The rivalry between East Coast and West Coast US rappers escalated into mutual animosity in the early '90s, when the, initially purely artistic, skirmishes resulted in a struggle for influence over the ever-growing rap music market.

After a successful wave of gangsta rap records, the West had a slight upper hand and did not lose the initiative. After the breakup of the local *N.W.A.*, *Dr. Dre* did not hesitate for long and dropped a real bomb on the world. Filled with relaxed beats and samples from classic funk and soul records, his acclaimed solo album *The Chronic* laid the foundation for the sound known as 'g-funk'. He, thus, determined the music direction of the hip-hop mainstream for the next few years. *The Pharcyde*, on the other hand, brought some light into the dark corners of hip-hop's image, fuelled by gangsta rap. On their album *Bizarre Ride II the Pharcyde*, the four rappers try to compete who had the funniest thing happen to them, complain about their mums, and, now and then, have a serious think. They point out that not every time you go out into the streets at night, you are likely to get a good beating, or witness a violent crime. Sometimes, you manage to just hang out with your friends, goof around, talk nonsense, and have lots of fun doing it.

Despite their New York origins, *Beastie Boys* weren't exactly the epitome of East Coast rap; instead, they played in a league of their own. On their album *Check Your Head*, they took note of the newly stricter legal conditions of dealing with samples and were, thus, not caught off guard. They thought back to their hardcore punk beginnings, picked up their instruments once again and recorded all the musical material themselves. The resulting cocktail of rap, beats with elements of funk, jazz, rock, and guitar sound fit perfectly into the contemporary atmosphere of enchantment with alternative music.

The explosion of alternative culture had not only affected the broadcasting of radio and music television stations. When the film director Cameron Crowe decided to set the story of his new film *Singles* (1992) in Seattle, he provided significant space for the local music community. He used a lot of music by local bands and members of some of them even made cameo appearances in the film.

Surprisingly, the soundtrack was released a few months before the film was premiered in cinemas, taking advantage of the massively growing wave of interest in the Seattle scene. It contained new, or previously unreleased, material by *Alice In Chains*, *Soundgarden*, *Pearl Jam*, and *Mudhoney* and, almost immediately, became a hit. This approach changed the usual view of film music, as it also works really well independently of the film as a complete, self-standing compilation. Ultimately, the music component completely overshadowed the film itself; only a few would remember the details of the romantic plot and the relationships between the individual characters. Much more memorable was the scene with the members of *Pearl Jam* watching, with interest, a nature documentary about bee reproduction, Chris Cornell nodding appreciatively to a song that one of the heroes used more than successfully to test the output of the sound equipment in the car, or a close-up showing the cheerful face of *TAD*'s frontman at the least expected moment.

Another film, *1991: The Year Punk Broke* (1992) was only released in clubs, but was no less attractive to the alternative nation. A documentary showing *Sonic Youth* on their European tour, during which they shared the stage with *Nirvana*, *Dinosaur Jr.*, or *Babes in Toyland*, is a collage of concert shots, backstage interviews, funny moments, and silly non-jokes. It shows the joys and pitfalls of life on tour to the audience, but it is also interesting from the historical viewpoint. It captures the audience's authentic reactions to *Nirvana*'s performances just weeks before the release of *Nevermind* changed not only the lives of the band themselves, but also millions of fans worldwide.

The American alternative invasion also met with a favourable response in Great Britain and the rest of Europe. In fact, so favourable that it overshadowed domestic events for a while. Those who dictated the music trends of 1992 symbolically closed out the rock festival in Reading, England, with bands from Seattle dominating. However, this in no way meant that nothing interesting was happening in the British rock field.

After a series of well-received singles and with claims of the best rock album of all time, *Manic Street Preachers* burst onto the scene. On their first, very long-playing, record, *Generation Terrorists*, they oozed punk energy, irritated with their glam image, provoked with political lyrics and, above all, entertained with driving and melodic songs. Over time, *Generation Terrorists* is remembered as one of the most distinctive British debuts of the '90s.

Seasoned bands also produced excellent recordings. The stylish brothers of *The Jesus and Mary Chain* had some work to do after their not-so-convincing last album. On their new record, *Honey's Dead,* they remembered how to write really catchy songs and strummed their guitars with vigour. Even though the lead single from it was rejected by the legendary TV program 'Top of the Pops', produced by the BBC, due to its slightly controversial lyrics, the album still earned a nomination for the Mercury Prize, established that very year. *The Cure*, on the other hand, were to overcome the burden of expectations about how they would follow up on their two masterpieces from the previous decade. Once again, they looked profusely into the gloomy depths of the human soul, where their stories full of sadness and hopelessness originated, but they also, surprisingly, showed their friendlier face. The *Wish* album did not quite fulfil the wishes of the band's dark army of die-hards, but it climbed to the very top of the British album chart, in America, missing it by just a single hair from Robert Smith's famous haircut.

Looking back at British rock would not be complete without a mention of the 'Shoegaze' scene. It got its name from guitarists who stared down checking the many guitar pedals and effects at their feet during concerts. They used these in abundance to achieve stunning noise waves as well as a subtle psychedelic haze in which they enveloped their compositions, using ethereal vocals and dreamy melodies to create a specific sound.

It was in this period that the popularity of shoegaze culminated, supported by several additions to the genre's discography. After four mini-albums, *Lush* finally dared to record a long-player. They did not spare any of their typical ingredients on it; *Spooky*, thus, overflows with the sound of ringing guitars, bursts of unbridled energy and sweet co-vocals. Once caught in their enticing nets, you can be sure it will take a pretty long and nice time to get out of them. In contrast to the past, on their second record, *In Ribbons*, *Pale Saints* devoted themselves less to studio experiments; instead paying more attention to the songs themselves. In the new line-up, strengthened by a female vocalist and a second guitar, their expressive palette blossomed and, at the same time, enabled them to achieve a more complex noise painting in loud passages. This all resulted in one of the most varied collections born into the genre that year.

Critical voices, complaining about all the shoegaze bands sounding the same, might have been confused while listening to *Curve*'s debut. Programmed electronic beats, seeping through thick layers of distorted guitar tracks on *Doppelgänger*, pump an extra dose of adrenaline into the songs. Above this mass of sound, a dreamy voice floats, in places having an almost industrial touch, which balances the recording into an attractive whole. In spite of their attempts at sound innovation, shoegaze bands soon faded into the periphery of music columnists' interest as another passing fad.

At the beginning of the '90s, various forms of electronic music began to appear more and more in the music charts, although radio stations practically did not play it. Its countless offshoots and sub-genres found a fertile ground in dance clubs, as well as at clandestine parties organised throughout the country. Initially taking place in various abandoned warehouses, but gradually also in increasingly large open spaces, 'rave' parties reached multiple thousands of visitors and provided unmistakable evidence of the lively happenings on the electronic scene.

It was at one of these events that the producers from *Opus III* met their enigmatic singer, and their first joint single, *It's a Fine Day*, made fans dance all over the world. They also decorated the rest of their *Mind Fruit* album with clever production, accented with pop elements, showing, in an accessible form, many curious listeners what 'house' sounds like. *The Prodigy* chose a much more uncompromising approach. On their debut *Experience*, they avoided light melodic vocals; instead, they proved their excellent ear and sense for catchy samples, punctuating their wild 'breakbeat hardcore'. Nothing was sacred to them; they just as happily distilled from hip-hop and funk as from radio plays or educational films for children. Just for a change, they spiced up their memorable hit *Out of Space* with an old reggae record from the '70s.

The Orb explored the calmer waters of 'ambient' in their work. The first single *Blue Room* from their album *U.F.Orb* took sales up to number eight on the singles chart. At just under 40 minutes, the single is the longest track to ever do so. Based on this success, they were invited to perform a shortened version of the piece on the TV show called Top of the Pops, known, among other things, for its performers not playing live. *The Orb* dealt with the situation in their own way. Instead of simulating a live performance, they chose to play a game of chess on live TV while their music video played in the background.

Before long, electronic music was supposed to interfere more significantly in the direction of the mainstream. For the time being though, the videos of electronic artists were used to, occasionally, provide variety to MTV's prime time. The time to compete for awards at the Video Music Awards was yet to come. The year 1992 was clearly marked by alternative rock, and this was duly reflected in the course of this anniversary event. *Red Hot Chili Peppers* received a total of nine nominations for two of their clips and took home three awards, others going to *Nirvana*, *Metallica*, and *The Cure*. How these bands were an alternative to the mainstream was mainly shown by their live performances.

That night, a few of them faced off on stage with such big stadium attractions as *Def Leppard*, *Guns 'n' Roses*, and *U2*, who put on their signature spectacular show. *Nirvana*, first, tried the nerves of the event producers with the opening notes of *Rape Me*, a piece they were expressly forbidden to play, before they started *Lithium*. At the end of it, Krist Novoselic fumbled with his own bass, which subsequently knocked him to the ground, and he staggered backstage with his head in his hands. Meanwhile, his two colleagues were smashing up their equipment on stage and provoking Axl Rose of *Guns 'n' Roses*.

Their Seattle rivals from *Pearl Jam* assaulted the audience with a shower of undiluted emotions in the ecstatically gradated song *Jeremy*, as the otherwise calm guitarist Stone Gossard lost his self-control and the singer Eddie Vedder's intensely dramatic performance sent shivers down everybody's spines. *Red Hot Chili Peppers* turned the stage into one big loose party, where, in the swirling mass of dancing bodies, it was easy to lose track of who was a performer and who was the audience. Alternative bands offered their rock fans the opportunity to experience spontaneity, believability, and the magic of unpredictability, should they have been tired of rehearsed gestures, choreography, and contrived theatre, calculated for effect.

The award for best video by a new artist as well as best alternative video went to *Nirvana*. Samuel Bayer shot the unforgettable visual accompaniment to their song *Smells Like Teen Spirit* as his first ever music video. With it, he began a respectable career of over 20 years, as one of the most prominent creators of music videos.

He moved from the painting canvas to the director's chair, which was reflected in his expressive visual style and a sense of shot composition and artistic stylisation. He not only directs his works but also personally takes care of the lighting and camera work. On the list of fifty artists with whom he has cooperated, such names can be found as *David Bowie*, *Metallica*, *Garbage*, *The Jesus and Mary Chain* or *Marilyn Manson*, and he has put his name to such classic *pieces as Bullet With Butterfly Wings by The Smashing Pumpkins, No Rain by Blind Melon* and *Zombie by The Cranberries*. Just like many of his colleagues, his next steps led him to shooting commercials, where he was able to use his experience with the short dynamic visual form. Also in this field, he collected several awards for his work for such brands as *Nike* or *Mountain Dew*. A significant part of his portfolio consists of advertisements for car manufacturers like *Nissan*, *Lexus*, *Chrysler*, and others.

His ability to capture a disturbing atmosphere and specific work with light did not go unnoticed by the producers of the remake of the famous slasher horror *A Nightmare on Elm Street* (2010). Initially, he twice rejected the offer to direct it, but finally accepted the challenge. Although the film was ranked among the most commercially successful remakes of the genre, critics were not exactly thrilled. The trailer for the upcoming film *Icarus Rises* suggests that, in Samuel Bayer's case, the smell of gasoline and love of engines goes further than just a short commercial. A new picture from his studio could, thus, be a real thrill ride and feast for the senses, just like we are used to from his music videos.

The following pages feature video clips shot in support of singles released in 1992.

Selected and commented on by:
~ Shezz, + Zebra, # Aran, * Rasťo, ‡ Veni, ° Iva, × Kubsson,

The Cure - High   *

This was the last album on which The Cure managed to keep their inimitable sound. They were the masters of bittersweet moods, perfect guitar melodies, and Robert Smith's voice was able to permanently etch into your soul. Thanks to my brother, this band was the soundtrack to my childhood, and they taught me that even sadness can be beautiful.

Rage Against the Machine - Freedom   ~

"Is it Rock? Is it Rap? Is it Grunge?" No, it's RAGE! The first time I heard them, I fell in love with not only them, but also the drums. Been playing ever since, and this still inspires me today. Grab a beer, let your hair down, turn it up to 11, and run around your home screaming. Well, this is what I do.

Morrissey - We Hate It When Our Friends Become Successful

The first bigger hit for Moz when using Alain Whyte as co-writer. Ingeniously true song title and one of my most favourite Morrissey lyrics of all time. What more could one wish for? Yes, I am one of those who enjoy 'Moz's' solo career more than 'The Smiths'.

Kyuss - Green Machine   +

A desert, the stars and rock'n'roll. A stellar single from the second album of this stoner/desert rock band, written by the drummer Brant Bjork. Josh Homme (of Queens of the Stone Age fame) creates the unmistakeable thumping Kyuss sound with his down-tuned guitar through a bass amp. Do not underestimate the desert dryness. Listen with a chilled beer!

4 Non Blondes - What's Up   ~

First song I learned to play on guitar, and still the only song I can play without checking chords. My baby sister loved this as it became her lullaby song; I played it to her every night to help her sleep. Luckily, I did not play her this video every night; I imagine she would have grown up differently if I had.

Pantera - Mouth for War   *

I have watched this video a hundred times with fascination. Phil Anselmo is, at first sight, a bloke who you hope will not ask you for a cig when you see him. But even so, you cannot take your eyes off him, like a rabbit in the headlights of a speeding car. The extreme mix of aggression and dangerous charisma which defined Pantera's music can also be heard in this song.

Stone Temple Pilots - Creep ~

Take a slice of Pearl Jam, add a slab of Nirvana, sprinkle on some Alice in Chains, then stick it all in Soundgarden bread. You now have the perfect grunge sandwich, which STP are. A unique band that comprised every element of the Seattle sound, but yet remained so individual. This song defines Acoustic Grunge.

Rein Sanction - Every Color

'The first band on Sub Pop whose record ended up being reduced', my friend and witness to this, Standa Procházka, wrote about them on Twitter some time ago. And perhaps the most timeless band on Sub Pop overall. Because, if Rein Sanction released their records from the '90s today, nobody would notice the difference. A knotted, mysterious, introverted, and stirring band.

Ani DiFranco - In or Out +

Sexuality is often a difficult thing. With the American songwriter, poet, and great guitar player Ani DiFranco, this theme has resonated since puberty. But only in this song did it get her full attention, in which she openly describes the thoughts of a woman who considers herself bisexual. And what about you? Do you feel In or rather Out?

Faith No More - A Small Victory   +

Apart from regular drills in the gym, having a father who is a coach also brings some positives to one's life. He engraves in you a desire and, later, also the will to win. As you're growing up, you realise not all fights can be won. In the beginning, it annoys you fundamentally but, with passing time, you reconcile with that fact and can even enjoy small victories.

The Lemonheads - It's a Shame About Ray   *

Former punks who now wear laundered shirts, wash their hair and their singer is a model?! Well, this is something of a 'guilty pleasure'. I just guzzle up those very short ultra-melodic songs and the sweet vocals. It is like dessert after a good lunch – eat too much, and it might upset me, but in the right amount, it is pure joy.

Carter USM - The Only Living Boy in New Cross   ~

The transition period between late '80s and early 90's can clearly be heard. Just enough power chord guitar, and vocals to set off any youngster, whilst still having the electronic keyboards and pop element to have an '80s undertone feel. Lyrics so good, if they were written on pink paper, would make a wonderful poem.

Nick Cave and The Bad Seeds - Straight to You

This song comes from the best album by Nick Cave. An awesome performance from The Bad Seeds, great songs, and brilliant shows. 'Straight to You' is one of the best love songs from the first half of the '90s which is accompanied by a TOTALLY bizarre video – I'm still not sure what to make of it. Unfortunately, Cave hasn't managed to create anything this powerful since.

Tori Amos - Winter   +

A Magnum Opus. The clearest mountain spring which quenches every thirst. An untameable flame that ignites the extinguished candle in us. A song which carries an infinite intimacy, interwoven by the very fragility of being. The silence in the midst of freshly fallen snow. Let this Winter in and it warms you up with such heat that only Tori can radiate.

Biohazard - Punishment   *

Not many nice things are said about New York's Brooklyn. That's exactly where Biohazard come from. A pissed-off gang; putting anything other than musical instruments in their hands is a disaster waiting to happen. A mixture of metal, hard-core, rap, and choruses that would drive a crowd in the pit nuts. The toothless grin of Billy Graziadei warns – this will shift your threshold of pain.

Manic Street Preachers - Motorcycle Emptiness *

There are certain songs for which one listen was enough to re-member them forever. From some of them, I remembered a guitar riff, from others, it was the chorus or at least a piece of a verse. These fragments then spontaneously surface in the magic jukebox of my mind and, in unexpected moments, season my life. This one is playing in my head right now.

Alice in Chains - Down In A Hole ~

Some songs speak to you; some shout at you, but this one squeez-es my heart. Every word sung strikes me with the honesty and pain intended. Just listening to this song can instantly change my mood, make me happier, or more reflective, or surprise me and take me somewhere I was not expecting. Instrumentally beautiful.

Cows - Mine

Cows – not only one of the most lunatic bands on Amphetamine Reptile but also of the whole rock history. Only a few could fit so many perverted riffs, anger, frustration, but also detachment and irony in their songs. And the record 'Cunning Stunts' is the best act of the whole of Cows' catalogue. The golden age of AmRep… Mine!

Inspiral Carpets - Two Worlds Collide   +

The lyrics 'try too hard' in several places but, otherwise, it is a beautifully naive song about where this world is heading and how people can be so blind towards the suffering of others. Let's feel a bit down and think about ourselves and where our lives are going. A headstrong Madchester band with typically subtle psychedelia in their sound. Mightily singable!

Urge Overkill - Girl, You'll Be a Woman Soon   ~

When this song starts to play, it takes me back to a cinema, lying about my age to try and watch an 18, as a 14-year old, and that thrill of getting in still excites me. So, to state the obvious, it makes up a great soundtrack, and this song will live on through that, however, never overlook how good this is, even without it.

House of Pain - Jump Around   *

"I would NEVER listen to hip-hop as there are no guitars nor proper singing, so why would I?" (Me, 1992). Then this track came along, and I understood what a mess a good beat can make. I did indeed jump as Everlast ordered; that is an absolute fact. A party anthem that indelibly placed hip-hop on my musical map.

Body Count - There Goes the Neighborhood ~

For those easily offended, please take no further action. For those with a passion for rock, thrash metal or hardcore punk; please immerse yourself into this world of hurt. Colourful language and in-your-face bluntness that would cause most to curl up and cry, Body Count take no prisoners; welcome to their neighbourhood.

The Breeders - Safari

This video immediately caught my attention. The women are dressed like teachers from a primary school and it's a totally weirdly constructed song. Where is the verse, where is the chorus, and where do they both continue? The Breeders had an advantage in the post-Pixies hysteria but, in the space of approximately twenty years, it is clear that this band hadn't 'aged' as much as Pixies had.

Soul Asylum - Somebody To Shove +

Soul Asylum are an alternative pure-breed with melodic punk-rock in their blood. In spite of that, lots of people I know can only recall one thing when their name is mentioned – 'Runaway Train'. As if they were just another one hit wonder band. I'll convince you they are not! Forget the train. Let's take a ride in a Mustang and, along the way, we'll give someone a proper nudge and knock them off the road!

R.E.M. - Drive +

Sex, drugs and rock'n'roll. A cloak strewn with irony, which dresses you without you noticing. What was once a game held tightly in your hands turned you into a helpless puppet in a play later. No one will tell you where to go or what to do. It happens to you, and yet outside of you at the same time. A ride time can only stop. Tick-tock, tick-tock.

Sugar - If I Can't Change Your Mind *

Bob Mould has the gift to write a melodic song that sticks in your head and won't leave you alone for the rest of the day. He had already proved it in his previous band, the legendary, albeit underrated, Hüsker Dü, but only with Sugar did he finally receive the deserved attention. This song is so catchy and light-hearted that, for quite a while, you won't even realise it's actually about a breakup.

Opus III - It's A Fine Day ~

The DJ finishes the song and starts to mix in the next, the crowd hold their breath, hoping this is the tune they have been waiting for. We all have songs we know we should not like and keep quiet about, and this is one, but I'd admit to all how much I like it. Is she sexy or just from the '90s? You decide!

Mňága a Žďorp - Někdy °

Everyone has their own special reason to like this band. For me, it is their capability to harshly and honestly reveal the volatile feelings of someone living in the battleship greyness of this world – a sad optimist, a momentarily lost soul, an eternal doubter, and an occasional finder. And, also, the determination to, despite everything, give the world a chance again and again.

Screaming Trees - Shadow of the Season +

The Godfathers of the grunge scene. The deepness of the voice of the 'King of Shadows', who has never been embraced by the sun, happiness, or joy. Always walking on the dark side of the path of life, he asked the Lord to indulge him with what he desires for. The Lord offered him pain and suffering. Mark and his apostles listened to the Lord and passed his gifts to all mankind. Through their music.

Megadeth - Symphony of Destruction *

Most bands would sell their souls to the Devil in order to achieve what Megadeth has. They will, however, never make their peace with a thrash metal 'Number 2'. Although they made it to a significant second place of the album charts with their record 'Countdown to Extinction', this piece proves they were rightfully thinking of higher grounds.

Sublime - Date Rape   *

Punks, skaters, and surfers all loved Sublime. They attracted them with an irresistible mix of ska and reggae, whilst also confessing their punk roots. Their reputation of being a unique live act is also proven by this song. And whoever might have had naughty thoughts looking at the sexy chick in the bar is likely to forget all about them once they've heard the lyrics.

Blind Melon - Change   ~

Another great band touched by tragedy. Listen to this beautiful song, but don't get used to its style. Not all BM songs have this set up, but the acoustic ones are my personal favourite, as it shows off the 'hippie' vocals better. Those early nineties memories come flooding back when listening to this classic.

Leonard Cohen - The Future   ×

A personal sorrow archivist, a relay runner between the highlights and disappointments of life. A poet who started to sing and his voice turned into velvet. A singer who writes poems. In his hat, he warns us against a future full of ourselves. Are we listening to him, or just reaching our hands for the scraps of illusive happiness? The closing time is nigh.

Dr. Dre - Let Me Ride   +

The sunny streets of L.A., polished luxurious wheels, and beautiful girls shaking their graceful hips. Today it is such a cliché, but in the '90s this could not be missing from a proper rap video. Now add some good old funk enriched with hip-hop beats. Dr. Dre has space for all in his wheels and he'll be happy to give you a ride. Just let him drive.

Soul Asylum - Runaway Train   ~

I was always so keen to move to the next step in my life without enjoying the moment, except when listening to this. It acts as a trigger that brings such good memories, it grabs me and makes me want to return to my youth to live it all over again but, like most, I'm sure it's better in my mind than it actually was.

NOFX - Stickin' in My Eye   *

An institution of independent punk rock back at a time when Fat Mike would still pass as just Mike, and it was still sort of possible to navigate through their giant discography, and their songs were longer than the sprightly banter between them at concerts. Faster than fast, more entertaining than entertaining and, sometimes, more embarrassing than embarrassing. But always their own.

The Prodigy - Out of Space ~

My teenage years' soundtrack includes this song. It made me realise I do not 'have' to like only one kind of music. They had such catchy songs, but without being cheesy. They created a genre of music that bands still try to emulate today. Some songs make you tap your toes, some move your head, but this makes you dance!

Love Battery - Out of Focus *

They were from Seattle, they had guitars and the 'Sub Pop' logo on their releases. That was almost enough for a ticket to the big league at the beginning of the '90s. Even though music critics praised 'Dayglo', it was their only 15 minutes of fame. They swore their allegiance to fuzzy psychedelic guitars rather than trendy grunge riffs, so they remained unfairly underrated.

Nine Inch Nails - Wish +

The chilly atmosphere of a doorway to hell. A grey blue haze wraps the outline of a band in a giant cage. A mass of once-people craves to tear at their bodies and devour their energy from the intimidating closeness. Trent Reznor is throwing away the masks he got on his way to hell. He remains naked to the bone. He only wants one thing. To find something real and true.

Rage Against the Machine - Killing In The Name +

Rage itself did not descend from the heavens. It has not spurted up from fiery hell either. It was born here, on the Earth, in this system we live in. It stirs us through an anthem of resistance, able to set a wildfire even in a broken soul full of resignation. Its shine will forever illuminate the truth about killing in the name of values, which are but a mask of purpose for the executors.

Swans - Love of Life *

Swans' music is exciting and disconcerting at the same time; this band can merge the beautiful with the unpleasant in an engrossing way. This hypnotic mantra declaimed by Michael Gira's deep voice accompanied by Jarboe's pagan ritual vocals suggests that your relationship with them will not just be casual. Either for life, or not at all.

Stereo MC's - Step It Up ~

Release this song today, and it would be a number one hit. A timeless classic; which cannot be defined by a genre. A surprisingly good live act that never really made it big, but their few big hits have helped them remain today. Not many people know all the lyrics, but we all know the chorus, so sing along!

Jesus Lizard - Gladiator *

Imagine the 10 craziest things a singer could do on stage. David Yow of Jesus Lizard came up with twice as many long before you did. Of course, easier when this kind of band had his back! A crashing rhythm section and ingenious attacks of abrasive guitar will trample you down without remorse while the mic is ruled by an unchained Madman.

Sugarcubes - Hit +

Sweet as a sugar cube. Melts on your tongue. When I heard this song for the first time, I was immediately possessed by that voice and then had to hunt it down. A funk guitar accompanies captivating vocals and an unforgettable melody. Those were my key words for the shop assistant in the cult Roxy Music shop. After I hummed it, he got it, and knew I was looking for this Hit.

The Cure - Friday I'm In Love ‡

Those luckier ones of us can fall in love a few times a day and forget the new love in no time. Robert Smith was not that lucky, he could only do so on Fridays. But thankfully, he still wrote an outstanding song, which will force you to smile as if you were freshly in love. Recommendation: Enhance the bass during reproduction.

L7 - Pretend We're Dead   *

These four Amazonians do not rely on typical womanly weapons. They found themselves in simple raw riffs ingrown into a thick grunge sound, lyrics without constraints and singing without embellishments. They understood where their strength is and, with every subsequent record, they searched for the perfect mix from their arsenal. The album this song is from is their triumphant war cry.

Beastie Boys - Jimmy James   ~

Sometimes it's hard to distinguish between some rappers' voices, but never Beastie Boys. The music samples are never overused and arranged in a way like only an artist could. When I listen, I can smell New York and its subways and food stands. And how to make it smell a little sweeter, add a hint of Hendrix.

Helmet - Unsung   *

Helmet's music is like a punch to the face. It will either knock you down immediately or deliver the force which causes an explosion. Massive walls of start-stop riffs, a precise machinelike rhythm and distinctive vocals, unexpectedly civil, but quietly more dangerous. Like a guy who does not need to be intimidating, he can just stare. And whatever he thinks, he means.

King's X - Black Flag   +

King's X should not be pigeon-holed. They love hard rock, heavy metal, but you will also find they do blues, prog-rock, and psychedelia. In the song Black Flag, they ride the then current grunge wave. Spiritual lyrics and a bizarre video full of symbolism will hit everyone who has at least once had to look at the world through a black veil.

Ugly Kid Joe - Cats In The Cradle   ~

A cover song that's as good as the original; it happens, but not that often. A song about fatherhood, which not only fathers can relate to, but sons also. As I am about to become a father myself, I understand this message and its warning. A simple chord pattern and structure but put together in a genius way.

Bettie Serveert - Kid's Allright   *

This song exceedingly breathes of rehearsal space. The walls are resurfaced with egg boxes, the room is a pleasant working mess, and there is a relaxed atmosphere. "Shall we try the new one?" There's tension from being unrehearsed and, at the same time, certainty that it's not a big deal, as another thousand takes are available. Just because of that, it works right the first time, and everyone is somehow clear that it can't be done any better.

Sonic Youth - Youth Against Fascism ~

Bruised and battered instruments can still make a sound, and Sonic Youth can take a guitar, then smash a screwdriver into it, and make it sound wonderful. Rarely has a band confused me so much, is it so simple I could do it? Or is it in fact genius? I love listening to this song whilst debating this over and over.

Pale Saints - Throwing Back The Apple *

Even though life is not black and white, we often have to face an either-or choice. The apple of knowledge does not come with a price tag and we are to decide whether to taste it or not. Whatever happens cannot be undone and it doesn't help if we throw it away. I was curious to find out what Pale Saints sound like and I have now not listened to anything else for a week. May it always turn out this well.

James - Born Of Frustration +

If the producer had left you in the middle of recording, you might have written something similar to what James did. Although the lyrics do not indicate it at all, the song is amazingly playful. It is full of beautiful trumpet parts and has the perfect Brit-rock sound. I listen to it when I am sick and tired, and I cannot find a bucket.

Stone Temple Pilots - Plush +

Since I have known of STP, besides their inclination to grunge, I have also always been fascinated by their sense for melody. Be it Robert DeLeo's guitar riffs or Scott Weiland's undisputable feeling for vocals, I just enjoyed sinking into their exceptional songs; such I will never grow tired of. Only time will tell if they can ever create anything more famous than this one.

Buffalo Tom - Taillights Fade *

An album which every band waits for. A record where suddenly all the pieces of the puzzle naturally click into place and the band creates its masterpiece. Straightforward rockers and ballads with pieces of their heart wrapped into a jangly guitar sound, it is all there. It's a shame the audience were not paying attention... Fix it!

Faith No More - Everything's Ruined ~

I saw FNM live a few years ago and because of that, 'Everything's Ruined' for me. No band I ever see again will be as good as they were that night. Mike Patton is looking very young in this video, but he still has that unique voice and style. Bands to see before you die; FNM should be at the top of that list.

Front Line Assembly - Mindphazer   *

A thrilling video by the legends of industrial electronic, a throwback to action movies from the '80s and to nights spent in front of the computer in the entrapment of shoot'em ups. Diluted dialogues and dense action. Get armed to the teeth and erase everything, including the final boss. Driven by a boisterous soundtrack which pumps adrenaline into my veins, I have him in my crosshairs already.

Neil Young - Harvest Moon   +

This is how I imagine the evening when I am old, well, older. The right woman in my arms, an unfinished drink on the table, my heart full of tenderness, and a full moon in the sky. There is nowhere to rush, time has stopped, and the night pretends it will last forever, although we both know it might not. Neil Young will peacefully take us to that place where the morning begins.

Blind Melon - No Rain   *

I was fifteen; a young, restless and sad grunger, but I wasn't ashamed of it. With all my might, I tried not to like this song, as it was so catchy and had a positive vibe, the bee looked like my schoolmate D., their video was colourful and shiny and the band seemed in a good mood. Didn't work out, I still love it nowadays, and I'm not ashamed of it.

Suicidal Tendencies - I'll Hate You Better   *

'The Art of Rebellion' is perhaps the most musically diverse of ST's attempts. After their hardcore punk early days and following a thrash metal era, they recorded an album where they tried anything possible with gusto. As often happens, the only thing this most known and amazing song shares with the typical sound of theirs is probably the sarcasm in the lyrics.

Basehead - Not Over You   *

You can have talent, artistic vision, and enough determination to make it a reality and the world still just yawns and turns its head away because you're a few years ahead of your time. Basehead could talk the talk. Not enough rock, not quite hip-hop, not enough soul, not quite funk. An unusual, elusive band.

Mudhoney - Suck You Dry   *

The first stars from Seattle, responsible for the emergence of the 'grunge' phenomenon. They came, shone … and left for a beer, as they couldn't care less about success or fame. Maybe that's why they're playing until the present day, with the same ironic grin and the same vigour. Their brilliant garage blasts brim with energy, twice as much when they're pouring on you from the stage.

Luscious Jackson - Daughters of the Kaos   *

What is there to be experienced that makes you compose something like this? Maybe a false move on the Mexican border resulting in an unexpected look into the eyes of a rattlesnake. Seconds go by anxiously, the rattle is upright in warning, even the slightest move might trigger an attack. The heart bangs its life beat and the nerves are tight like strings on a guitar of a mariachi, strumming nearby.

Alice in Chains - Would?   +

It would be an unforgivable sin for a grunger, now bald, who goes into hiding to caress his flannel shirt in the wardrobe at a cottage, not to dignify the memory of this titanic song. For me, it remains the top musical experience forever and one of the most powerful and important songs of the soundtrack to my youth.

Catherine Wheel - Black Metallic   *

Catherine Wheel were born from a passionate unity of 'shoegaze guitar surfs' and 'Britpop melodies'. From their parents, they inherited only the best; however, they were rather in the background than the spotlight. If you give them a chance, you will not regret it. 'Ferment' is one of the best guitar records you've never heard.

The Jesus and Mary Chain - Reverence   *

They were able to write a song in which the guitars squeaked with the intensity of a train braking. And right after that a pop melody sweeter than candy floss. But, although they managed to record really imposing guitar feedback and a provocative slogan in 'Reverence', thanks to the mightily contagious beat, it is actually a first-class pop song.

Codeine - Realize   *

If Chronos wears a t-shirt of his favourite band, then it's Codeine. They managed to express with their music a compelling definitiveness and endless patience, which only a master of time can rule with. They are like a granule in an hourglass of infinity, rushing nowhere, their every tone weighs an aeon and their every verse an epoch. There is never enough time, but there is still always plenty of time.

Babes in Toyland - Bruise Violet   *

To judge Kat Bjelland according to her image would be a serious mistake. Dyed hair and lipstick make her look like a baby-doll, but only until she starts to play. The fascinatingly harsh and uncompromising music of Babes in Toyland floors you and the vocals make your blood freeze in your veins. Try to cheat them and they will tear you up with their teeth. And then, they write you this song – something for you to remember them by.

Stereo MC's - Connected   +

A British rap. An alter-house rhythm that carries on its shoulders a croak of funk saxophone and wantonly rousing flute. The soul vocals will also caress you. The result is a synergy and timeless dance experience. So, if you are preparing a proper '90s party at your place, 'Connected' won't let you or your guests down, that's for sure.

Lush - For Love   *

If any band deserved the attribute 'lush', it would indeed be Lush. Subtle veils woven from airy guitar motives and a charming angelic two-part harmony could have awed you at first listen. And who are we kidding, it's not just their ethereal and dreamy music but also the poignant sex appeal of Emma and Miki one cannot resist.

Disposable Heroes of Hiphoprisy
- Television, the Drug of the Nation   *

More of a documentary with an insistent bass sound than a typical hip-hop video. A few facts and opinions about our beloved telly, delivered critically, smartly, and with detachment. The lyrics, which haven't grown old a single day, and the age suits so well to the beat. Now that you've seen, will you reach for a book, or a remote control?

Red House Painters - 24 *

With increasing age, we are often made to cut back on our life expectations, when our ideas diverge from reality when taking stock. Did we want too much, or is the right time still to come? Reaching the goal the right way is more important than getting there fast. That, however, usually requires tons of patience and acres of time.

Bad Religion - Atomic Garden *

If your mum saw the singer maybe she might say he is a looker but if your grandma saw their logo, she might be outraged. One of the bands you certainly recognise a few seconds in. Greg Griffin and his unmistakable voice, unique melodies, and urgently critical lyrics are in perfect unity with energetic punk rock of the Californian style.

The Lemonheads - Mrs. Robinson +

What lead the punk rockers The Lemonheads to put a new coat on this Paul Simon hit? Apparently, it was a coincidence and an artistic whimsy. The singer, Evan Dando, does not have much love for their own version really, and does not understand its success to this very day. But I stand up for their cheery pop punk cover, and, I like to listen to it much more than the original.

Frente! - Ordinary Angels *

When I see the label 'pop', my musical receptors unconsciously turn to the position 'maybe not'. When I hear a record like this, my receptors cheerfully flash 'yes indeed!' If this smartly written, playful, and witty music was the standard for pop production, I would listen to the radio more often and without any qualms of threat to my taste.

Nirvana - Sliver *

The legendary sweater, a dancing toddler, and a song about which I long believed was a cover version. With disarming effortlessness and detachment, Nirvana proves here why they were once the biggest rock band in the world. Kurt's charisma and the patented scream, Krist's ingeniously catchy bass and Dave's drum kit punishment will make that clear for you.

Ministry - Jesus Built My Hotrod *

Ministry do not hide their main intention, not even for a moment – to beat the brain out of your head whilst you dance wildly to the rhythm of their industrial pulse. The nervous energy of punkish dirty guitars and the booming of a production plant at its peak are the right addition to your new cybernetic implant.

1993

The Smashing Pumpkins

Björk

Jamiroquai

Suede

The Afghan Whigs

Lenny Kravitz

The Breeders

Wu-Tang Clan

Candlebox

The Cranberries

Bad Religion

Cypress Hill

Orbital

PJ Harvey

Tool

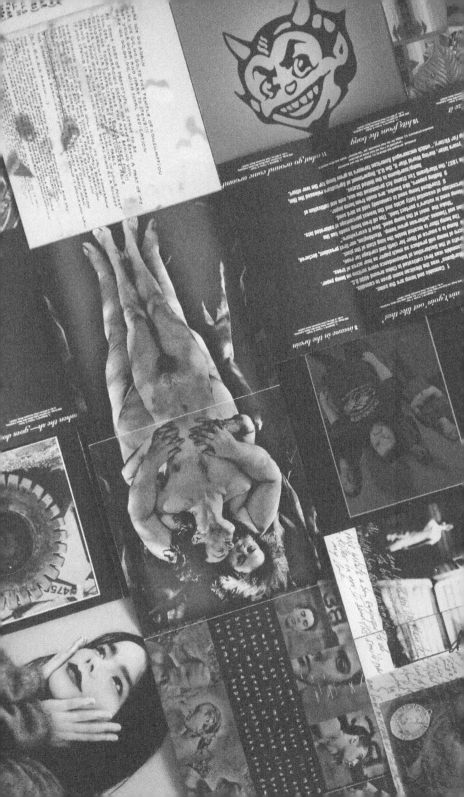

1993

The graceful ride of grunge gained in intensity and created space for other offshoots of alternative rock to come to the fore. Amplified guitar became part of the obligatory musical arsenal and the dynamic contrast between a quiet verse and a loud chorus became a standard element of any rock composition. Song lyrics were dominated by such personal themes as internal struggle, alienation from society, or soul-searching. Among many others, two distinct voices especially resonated in listeners' ears. With the media ready to get involved, fans were divided into two camps and music journalists liked to stir the dilemma of who is the voice of Generation X – Kurt Cobain or Eddie Vedder. The answer was to come soon, as both bands announced they were working on new albums. In just the first five days, *Pearl Jam* sold a dizzying 950,000 copies of their second album, *Vs.*, about five times more than the new release by *Nirvana*, whose record *In Utero* had come out about a month earlier. However, *Pearl Jam* appeared in the ten best-selling titles of the year with their album *Ten*, which they had released two years before. Thus, they suddenly had to deal with the status of the biggest American rock band, although barely three years had passed since they first played together live.

It was also thanks to them that Seattle continued to be a closely watched place. The aura of a guaranteed depository where bands with the umbrella label 'grunge' were to be found emboldened major record companies to venture into the local scene in an effort to find more golden nuggets.

Candlebox seemed one such band. Their music was based on traditional hard rock and relied on emotional vocals. They emerged at a time when the alternative revolution was slowly breaking out and the foundations of grunge had long been laid. But while they did not even try to fake their punk roots, their multi-platinum success launched a flood of accusations that they were not an authentic band and were just riding a fad. To this day, the best response to the haters is the power of the songs on their eponymous debut. On the other hand, *TAD* were among the long-term pillars of the scene, which is obvious from their first album for a major label. On their new release, they added a few melodic choruses and an excellent sound to the typically monstrous guitar riffs. *TAD* were, however, a band that had everything but luck on their side. An ill-advised poster promoting their European tour featured President Clinton with a conspicuous 'cigarette' in his hand and the caption read: "It's heavy shit". Not only did it cause them legal problems, but their publisher subsequently terminated their contract, despite the fact that their *Inhaler* album undoubtedly is heavy shit.

However, more than any other new band from Seattle, the expectations focused on in which direction *Nirvana* would proceed in their work. Die-hard fans were worried they might succumb to the temptation to satisfy the programmers of mainstream radio and strengthen their newly acquired star status. The band, however, had a different idea about their next steps. They did not bother too much with the recording, they banged out the whole album in two weeks. The producer was Steve Albini, known for his work with independent underground bands. *In Utero* is a dirtier, recognizably punkier, record than its trend-setting predecessor, which, as was to be expected, turned off those fans who discovered *Nirvana* through those ubiquitous hit singles. But those who appreciated the raw energy of their concerts welcomed the new record with enthusiasm.

It was not only Seattle that was full of musical talent, and not only grunge was on the agenda of the rock scene. For several bands, the label 'alternative rock' was too broad and bland; however, they stood out from other genre pigeon-holes due to their individuality.

Afghan Whigs had a hard time getting rid of the grunge stigma after two records for Sub Pop, although they refined their sound more and more on each subsequent record. Flashes of R&B and soul, as well as brutally honest lyrics delivered with devastating intensity, made them a disturbingly original band. The bare heart of the 'homme fatal' was the central theme of their breakthrough album *Gentlemen*. They had their pick of major record labels to choose from and they had already recorded this 'private exhibition of relationship hell' for one of them. *The Smashing Pumpkins* were another band for whom being connected with grunge was rather harmful. This was mainly induced by the frequent dynamic changes in their ambitious, prog-like, compositions and urgently personal lyrics. In order to realise their vision, the preparation of their second record, *Siamese Dream*, required three months of gruelling, rigorously precise, studio work layering countless guitar tracks and a generous recording budget. Bursts of thundering guitars alternating with sweetly melodic passages created a work of epic proportions, winning both passionate detractors and supporters.

On their new release, *Urge Overkill* drew from a completely different barrel. And it doesn't really matter if it was bourbon or port. In the mass of gloomy bands defining alternative rock in the first half of the '90s, it was impossible to miss their undisguised self-indulgence and cultivated image of rock stars, supported by the corresponding lifestyle. The exuberant atmosphere that emanated from *Saturation* proudly demonstrates the fact it was they who believed in their big rock'n'roll mystification the most.

The growing number of bands originating in the independent scene and suddenly releasing on major record labels was accompanied by heated debates and dissent within the ranks of the underground community. Strict advocates of 'do-it-yourself' ethics considered such actions a betrayal of the basic principles of the scene and, thus, a reason to stop supporting such bands. Some fans took the situation more kindly and waited to see how the resulting record would sound on the new label before passing judgment. One way or another, both camps still had enough options to agree on, as indie labels were still teeming with original bands.

Despite the sound trends, *Morphine*, a peculiar trio with no guitar but a proper dose of devilish charm instead, gained a legion of devoted followers. Their economical, yet imaginative, music was dominated by soul-speaking saxophone tones and first-class bass lines. They were just as able to wrap a jazz club audience around their finger as to bring rock fans to a boil, which is best evidenced by their second album, *Cure for Pain*. Another three-member line-up, *The Jon Spencer Blues Explosion*, did without a bass guitar for a change. 'Explosion' is the key word in their name, which is exactly what they sound like on *Extra Width*. Pieces of funk, blues, and rock'n'roll scattered and twisted by the explosion are welded together by the sound of two insanely frenzied guitars. These are hammered into desired shape by a drummer who had, undoubtedly, had experience in a blacksmith's workshop.

Bad Religion had been a hallmark of the highest punk rock quality since the early '80s, their seventh album, *Recipe for Hate*, also lived up to this reputation. Here, they slowed down a bit and tried a few new tricks, but still kept it within the boundaries of pure, melodic, and socially engaged punk rock. Shortly after its release, however, they moved to a major label and reissued the record. For many fans, the name, ironically, fulfilled its prophecy and became a reason to blacklist the band.

In spite of the fact that women had had their irrefutable place in rock music since its inception, their creative contribution had not received much attention. Rock'n'roll was considered a rather male domain. Topics addressed in the lyrics focused around the male view of the world, although women often entered them as a significant source of inspiration. For the time being, women mainly performed in bands as singers and, only to a lesser extent, as instrumentalists. This started to change in the first half of the 1990s when strong female authors emerged on both sides of the Atlantic, either as front people of bands or performing solo.

It takes a lot of self-confidence to leave a band acclaimed by both fans and critics due to a lack of space for self-expression. Kim Deal of *Pixies* was brave enough to do just that, and her *Breeders* exceeded all expectations. Musical playfulness, the desire to experiment, and the ability to compose a hit as if by chance turned their second album, *Last Splash*, into a platinum success. *Liz Phair* already impressed with her home-recorded demo tapes, and she did not mess around unnecessarily in the studio with her full-length debut, *Exile in Guyville*, either. With minimalist production, it was not only her catchy songs she made stand out, but especially her carefreely direct lyrics. In them, she gives a glimpse into the recesses of the female mind, which many others would not even reveal to their diary. *PJ Harvey*, back then still a trio, recorded a follow-up to their intense first record for a major label, but it is not obvious from their music. Sonically raw and emotionally stripped to the bone, *Rid of Me* kicks and scratches mercilessly, which makes it as much a physical as a cathartic experience.

Björk works with completely different means of expression. With the *Debut* album, she drew a thick line behind her past as a rock singer and opened the door to the world of boundless creativity that adorns her work. Her songs have the form of dance electronics, atmospheric trip-hop, and are also inspired by jazz, and her fans could only guess where she would go from there.

Most alternative music production carried a serious tone, reflecting the insecurity and distress of the adolescent youth. MTV fought against this trend when it brought out some proper puerility to the screens in the form of the animated series 'Beavis & Butt-Head'. The main characters, a pair of not so bright truants, experienced pleasures worthy of their intellect; peeing in the pool and throwing bugs into a deep fat fryer being among the less outrageous. MTV, thus, had to move the programme to night-time quite early on after its launch and show a disclaimer before its broadcast for the less understanding viewers that the characters are only cartoons and none of what they do is to be tried at home. Still, it did not take away from its popularity, most likely also thanks to the music it offered.

What Beavis and Butt-Head liked to do most was sit in front of the TV and comment on video clips. Their remarks were often bizarre, derogatory, always surprising, but mostly decadently funny. They mainly considered rock and metal music to be 'cool', which is why, out of the records released in 1993, *Tool* could not escape their attention. The evocative atmosphere of their first studio album *Undertow* is formed by a mix of dark metallic sound and persistent vocals pounding on those doors of the hidden chambers of the human psyche one would rather keep locked. The penetrating experience of the music is further enhanced by the whiplash stop-motion animated clips, abounding in horror elements. Of course, only until the moment when the two cartoon commentators turn them into a laughable farce.

They were also impressed by the deep voice of the singer of goth metal band *Type O Negative*. Despite the slow, heavy, and doom-covered songs on the *Bloody Kisses* album, which garnered them considerable attention, this band was known for its specific sense of humour. As they were happy enough to put a hairy detail of their frontman's backside on the cover of their previous record, it would be safe to say they were not offended by Beavis and Butt-Head's peculiar compliments.

Those music video fans who like to watch clips in their entirety and, preferably, without the constant sniping of two giggling teenagers were not probably best pleased with the Beavis and Butt-Head show.

However, if they lived in the US, the subscription edition of Rock Video Monthly VHS tapes must have filled them with unspeakable bliss. It started to come out in the first half of 1993 in the genre categories Pop, Rap, Alternative, and Heavy Metal. For a truly affordable price, the subscriber found in their post box a tape with ten videos of their favourite genre every month, even though there was no fixed system for classifying them according to music categories. Whether on purpose or due to inattention, it was nice how genre stereotypes were subverted when bands like *Stone Temple Pilots, Therapy?,* or *Rage Against the Machine* found themselves in the heavy metal category in a certain month, next time to appear on an alternative collection alongside *The Breeders, Live* or *Tori Amos.* These, however, might be seen next on a tape labelled Pop.

In contrast, the compilation released to mark the thirteenth anniversary of the 4AD label's operation was only available in Europe. *The 13 Year Itch* could only be purchased at one of the six birthday concerts held in London and the two thousand lucky owners of this limited edition found on it videos from then-current recordings by *Frank Black, His Name Is Alive, Lush, Red House Painters,* and others. At Sub Pop, they could not go without an ironic grin on the cover of the second part of the *Sub Pop Video Network Program,* when they aptly summed up the situation on the independent scene with the slogan "I scream, you scream, we all scream for a major label record contract". Apart from the recently departed *Afghan Whigs,* the next batch of video clips presented samples of another musical direction in the form of *Velocity Girl, Codeine, Pond,* and *Supersuckers.* The diverse mix of old familiars and new faces sent a clear message that there is no need to worry about the label's future.

Originally alternative music forms gradually became greater and greater part of mass popular culture. Film could not avoid this trend either. Production companies fully realised the promotional potential of the music video and its influence on a significant part of the youth population. The effort to encourage them to get off the couch and go to the cinema was reflected in the increased appearance of alternative bands on film soundtracks, as well as the production of music videos promoting specific films.

Last Action Hero (1993) is remembered as one of the biggest box office flops of '90s action films, and not even the muscular Arnold Schwarzenegger in the lead role could help it. The honour of the film is, thus, only saved by its stellar soundtrack. It portrays a period snapshot of the hard rock scene, capturing the generation of bands dictating current events such, as *Alice in Chains* and *Megadeth* side by side with the ageless stalwarts of *AC/DC* and *Aerosmith*. The film *So I Married an Axe Murderer* (1993) did not break audience records when released either. Although Mike Myers might have funnier characters to his credit, the music is yet more pleasantly surprising. The film makers mostly bet on the darlings of the British independent scene and gave *Ned's Atomic Dustbin*, *Suede*, and *The La's* a chance to shine.

However, *Judgment Night* would surely become the sovereign winner of the 1993 imaginary competition for a film overshadowed by its own soundtrack. Even Emilio Estevez himself might have forgotten that he starred in it. However, the unique concept of cooperation between rappers and rock bands, on which the soundtrack is based, has a lot to offer to this day. The ferocious intensity of the fusion of *House of Pain* and *Helmet*, the awe-inspiring brotherhood of *Onyx* and *Biohazard*, the narcotic-psychedelic trip of *Cypress Hill* and *Sonic Youth*, or the sheer joy of *De La Soul* and *Teenage Fanclub* joining forces are just a few possible approaches to bridging rock and hip-hop, as they were immortalised by this timeless soundtrack.

Several artistically prominent and commercially successful records from the previous period helped hip-hop to strengthen its position as one of the most influential musical and cultural phenomena of the '90s. Anyone who might have expected that it was just a fad that would soon die out, was put right by the musical events of the following years.

This dynamically developing genre gathered more and more supporters and kept finding enough fresh stimuli to keep its 'in' position. After a period of dominance by gangsta rap and g-funk from the West Coast, the other side also made itself known fairly strongly. On the East Coast, the inventive and cultured *A Tribe Called Quest* earned respect. Instead of street darkness or obsessing over who is the bigger gangster, they used penetrating intellect and a positive charge as their weapons, even when it came to serious topics. All of that was enhanced by delicate work with samples on their third record, *Midnight Marauders*, which deservedly became their most successful. *Wu-Tang Clan*, a nine-member commando unit with an unprecedented plan for total domination, literally took the stage by storm. During a five-year period, in addition to group efforts, they decided to send all members on a solo exploration and, literally, flood the scene with rap of the highest quality. The first proof that they meant it and it was not just a delusional vision of their exaggerated self-confidence was provided by their debut *Enter the Wu-Tang (36 Chambers)*. They caused a small earthquake in the hip-hop scene, but compared to what was still to come, it was but an innocent prelude.

On the West Coast, *Cypress Hill* emerged from a cloud of thick smoke for the second time. In the first week alone, their new album was bought by a quarter of a million fans who were wondering whether the boys still had the taste for it. They did not disappoint, *Black Sunday* is a mixture of intoxicating aroma and exotic accent in an irresistible ratio, and its concentrate, the immortal party track *Insane in the Brain*, sent dance floors mad all over the world.

Meanwhile, the British Isles were experiencing a musical identity crisis after being hit full force by the wave of American alternative rock. It flooded the pages of music periodicals, which, instead of the usual "new Beatles", were looking for a "new Nirvana". Expressive singing along with noisy guitars dominated the airwaves and represented the key to the attention of radio programmers as well as concert promoters. The decline in interest in British guitar bands was reflected in audience numbers at their concerts as well as record sales not only overseas, but also on home soil.

There, the recently celebrated Shoegaze scene ran out of steam. Although several of its representatives did not stand still and moved towards so far unexplored territories, due to the current musical climate, their efforts were usually not met with a warm response from the audience. The pensive *Slowdive* developed their dreamy music to somewhere on the border of a supersensual experience, i.e., at the completely opposite end of the sound spectrum from the location of the explosive and dynamic present. Critics at the time made them feel it; their ethereal record *Souvlaki* only received well-deserved recognition years later. *Swervedriver*, on the other hand, did not skimp on the decibels on their second studio record, *Mezcal Head*, and stepped more than lightly on the effect pedals. Their deep guitar massage, as well as their love for fast cars and powerful engines resonated especially with American listeners. The new release by *The Boo Radleys* was a generous feast for their listeners. At its seventeen-course menu, they could not help but marvel at the number of tempting ingredients stacked next to each other in a colourful sound puzzle on *Giant Steps*.

Blur completely broke away from the influence of shoegaze on their second record. When recording *Modern Life Is Rubbish*, they drew inspiration from the treasury of British guitar pop of the '60s. They made it clear from the bottom of their lungs what they thought of American musical supremacy and raised the flag of national pride, which an increasing number of followers were soon to start identifying with.

Although they were not setting the tone for world events in the rock field at the time, dance music was indisputably a British domain. The electronic scene was making itself known more and more prominently. Dance clubs were bursting at the seams while various originally secret or underground events were starting to be official in character. Producers of electronic music began to appear on the lists of performers at music festivals, gave public concerts, and the fact their records were climbing up the charts suggested the interest of increasingly wider audiences.

After their well-received debut, *Orbital* still could not come up with a better record name, even on the second try, than simply *Orbital*. The new album, full of complex acid house compositions, got to be called the 'Brown one' after the colour of its cover. It sold well despite *Orbital* being unofficially banned from Top of the Pops, one of the most powerful promotional tools of the time. They were among the first electronic bands that appeared on the programme. For their premiere in 1990, they dressed up in t-shirts protesting the then government's newly introduced 'poll tax'. In addition, when the producers of the programme did not allow them to play live, they moved around the stage in a bored manner and did not even try to pretend their keyboards were plugged in. Just to be on the safe side, they did not get invited for the next six years. *Saint Etienne* were much more accommodating. On TOTP, they enthusiastically performed two singles from their second album *So Tough*. On it, they presented their patented mix of dance beats and cute, catchy melodies. They interlinked the pieces with excerpts from movies which, together with the rich orchestral arrangements, enhanced the feeling of a soundtrack to a forgotten romantic story from somewhere deep in the '60s.

Jamiroquai's first long-playing release sent out completely different vibes. The less electronics hidden in the grooves of *Emergency on Planet Earth*, the more dance to be unleashed by their charge of acid jazz and funk fired by an ecological activist, a hat extremist, and a dance specialist behind the mic. Top of the Pops' viewers were able to see it with their own eyes, and the record eventually made it to the top of the British album chart.

Before this time, the top of the charts was ruled by several other bands that were to indicate the direction of British independent music in the near future. After a four-year hiatus and the bankruptcy of their home label Factory Records, *New Order* returned to the scene. The fans were lured to their sixth album *Republic* by the single *Regret*, containing all the band's usual trump cards – an unmistakable bass line, a hit chorus, and the potential to make anyone within reach dance. Although the album immediately shot to the top of the charts, it generated mixed reactions among fans. With the exception of the pilot single, the band almost completely abandoned their original sound, covering the live bass with layers of pulsing electronic beats and leaning more towards modern dance production.

A month earlier, the eagerly awaited, eponymous first record by *Suede* was released. It was preceded by rumours of the best new British band and a couple of singles. The third single in a row, *Animal Nitrate*, was premiered by the band during the prestigious Brit Awards. The glam rock theatricality and challenging stage performance of the extravagant singer impressed the audience like a bolt from the blue. However, it was mainly their melodic songs with poetic lyrics that breathe vice and an intimate knowledge of London life, thanks to which *Suede*'s debut sold at a tremendous speed, and today it is considered one of the originators of the music genre known as 'Britpop'.

It was *Depeche Mode* who vacated the top spot on the album charts for them. With their album *Songs of Faith and Devotion*, they confirmed that exceptional works are often created in borderline circumstances. The long months of recording irreversibly marked the relationships of the band members but stimulated them to an extraordinarily creative performance. They announced this dark record, enriched by experimentation with live instruments, with the almost rock single *I Feel You*, and set off on a mammoth tour lasting over a year. Two things were crystal clear at the end of it – who is the biggest synth pop band in the world and that no more music with the same line-up would be created.

On the back cover of *Songs of Faith and Devotion*, the Mute label logo stands out proudly. It was founded in 1978 in London by Daniel Miller, an ardent fan of the sound of synthesizers, as well as, at that time, still nascent electronic music. Originally, it was only to be used for the release of his own, self-recorded, single. Emboldened by the unexpected success of the record as well as the subsequent discovery of other musically related artists, he launched Mute as a regular label a year later.

The turning point in the label's history came when he signed a contract with *Depeche Mode*. From the beginning, their popularity grew with each subsequent record and spread beyond the borders of the British Isles. In an effort to give the band adequate support, the label expanded along with it. Daniel Miller recognised the importance of mutual loyalty in building a long-term relationship between the publisher and the artist. This approach bore him fruit. The artists remained loyal to the label even when more lucrative offers came knocking on their doors and, thus, helped it survive even during less favourable times. In the course of the '80s, Mute became one of the leading labels not only of synth pop, but also of experimental electronic music, not avoiding bands with traditional instrumentation either. From the fertile ashes of the wild post-punkers *The Birthday Party*, who recorded their last album under their banner, rose *Nick Cave* and his *The Bad Seeds*, as well as the no less harrowing *Crime & the City Solution*. After leaving *Depeche Mode*, Vince Clarke continued to churn out hits with *Yazoo*, while *Recoil*, *Alan Wilder*'s solo project, spun more demanding electronic textures. Nonetheless, they all continued to defend Mute's colours, where no one was favoured. The political provocateurs *Laibach*, the industrial noisemakers *Einstürzende Neubauten*, and the pioneers of electronic body music *Nitzer Ebb* all enjoyed equal attention. Regardless of the amount of expected sales or genre affiliation, the underappreciated dance floor burners *Renegade Soundwave*, the retro rockers of *Inspiral Carpets*, and the electronic sound magician *Moby* all worked side by side.

With regained independence, a sense of musical adventure never lost, and despite their name, Mute have something to say to this day.

Depeche Mode were, indisputably, the most successful band from the Mute 1993 catalogue, the year they managed to conquer the top of the album charts on both sides of the Atlantic for the first time.

Therefore, they could not be missing among the nominees at the annual MTV Video Music Awards. However, the awards were collected by others that year.

Pearl Jam, Nirvana, Alice in Chains, and *Stone Temple Pilots* split the awards between them in seven categories, confirming the unceasing popularity of grunge. Several of the performers prepared a few live surprises for the audience during the evening. *Lenny Kravitz* forever booked his place in the rock-world Pantheon with his anthem *Are You Gonna Go My Way*, and whoever did not realise it straight away after the sound of his electrifying guitar riff was, perhaps, convinced by *John Paul Jones* from *Led Zeppelin* guesting on bass. *Soul Asylum* played a soulful version of *Runaway Train*. *R.E.M.*'s *Peter Buck* played mandolin, *Victoria Williams* keyboards and the singer *Dave Pirner* donned his best pants for the occasion. *R.E.M.* significantly rearranged the song *Drive* which, in this form, later became a concert rarity sought after by fans. *U2* also performed in an atypical line-up. On their behalf, *The Edge* came to sit on stage and spoke the lyrics of the minimalist electronic mantra of *Numb*. In a world premiere by *Pearl Jam*, they presented the energetic new song *Animal* from their upcoming second record. They were soon joined by *Neil Young* to belt out his *Rockin' in the Free World*. He made everyone present feel that he could still teach the youngsters a few tricks when it comes to the intensity of guitar wailing.

For the video to their song *Jeremy*, *Pearl Jam* received three astronaut statuettes at the award ceremony. The singer *Eddie Vedder*, however, could not hide his mixed feelings. He expressed his doubts about the meaning and, especially, the feasibility of competitive comparison of works of art. In support of his words, the band did not make any videos for the next five years and decided to solely talk to their fans by means of their concerts.

The most 1993 MTV Video Music Awards (four in total) went to the song *Jeremy*. This moving story inspired by real events, impressively made into music by *Pearl Jam*, was brought to life by Mark Pellington.

The captivating execution won the band a prize in the Video of the Year category and Mark the award for best director.

He gained experience in combining image and sound in the MTV promotional department, where he started making TV shots, which is where the origin of his striking signature style also lies. With the help of snappy editing, he builds dramatic collages composed of unusual details, archival footage, and text references, often set in a mysterious environment. He used his ability to sense the mood of music and interpret it as a sequence of intuitive images when creating video clips. He recorded dozens of them for such bands as *Public Enemy*, *Alice in Chains*, *Screaming Trees*, *Silverchair*, *The Disposable Heroes of Hiphoprisy* or *Lush*. While being successful in the music industry, he did not begrudge television work either. In the documentary series *The United States of Poetry* (1995), which mapped modern American poetry, he uniquely combined the author's delivery of verse and spoken word with tight visual representation. His intimate documentary *Pearl Jam: Single Video Theory* (1998) was released in home video format on VHS tape. In it, he revealed to the fans the creative process of a band known for its reluctance to present itself in front of the cameras, directly from their rehearsal room.

He is no stranger to the big screen either. In the thriller *Arlington Road* (1999), he tried his hand at working with Hollywood stars and, later, Oscar winners Tim Robbins and Jeff Bridges. As assistant director of the *U2 3D* project (2007), he stood at the birth of a spectacular concert recording, which was notable for several firsts in the field of 3D digital film. Mark Pellington is still active so we will certainly hear his name in connection to music video for some time to come.

Na nasledujúcich stránkach nájdete videoklipy natočené na podporu albumov vydaných v roku 1993.

Vybrali a okomentovali:
~ Shezz, + Zebra, * Rasťo, × Kubsson,

Butthole Surfers - Who Was in My Room Last Night? *

If smoke comes out of the barman's bottle, don't drink whatever's in it. If the waitress has green lips and a poisonous smile, keep your hands off her. If the band playing is called 'Butthole Surfers', go to a different bar. Unless you like adrenaline, a ride with the pedal to the floor, and a proper dose of thundering riffs from a crappy garage. In that case, stay, you won't regret it.

The Breeders - Cannon Ball ~

More than just a great intro, but what an intro. More than just pretty girls, but what pretty girls. More than just a funky song, but what funk. An anthem from the '90s that brings back all those memories of carefree summers. With the amazing bass hook, easy to forget how great the drums and guitar are.

Hazel - Day Glo   *

I am enraptured by the sincerity and pure enthusiasm that just sparkles from Hazel. I trust every word from the singer, a bass player who is deep in his own world, and a drummer who enjoys her every single hit. And the dancing creations of a non-playing shaman? Indescribable. When watching this, I fancy starting my own band. This will be the first song we learn.

Orbital - Halcyon +

A young housewife who has finally decided to wash the dirty dishes. Everything would be like from a bad and boring advertisement for a detergent if there wasn't something different. A detergent with the brand name Orbital. It can be, like it is commonly known, intensely hallucinogenic. Washing dishes has never been so entertaining!

Snoop Doggy Dogg - Who Am I (What's My Name) ~

What is cool, and what is not? Well, the simplest way to be sure, see what Snoop thinks of it, and only then will you have the definitive answer. Back when he was unknown, he already showed maturity in his music whilst being new and fresh and ever since has been breaking ground, and smoking whatever grows from it too.

For Love Not Lisa - Slip Slide Melting *

This song got me right after the first listen. When the unreal chorus comes, after a crushing introductory riff and following an electrifying ride of a guitar coupling, I want to scream. A total celebration of drive and disposition. But the true highlight is a beautiful epic break, which sends shivers down my spine.

The Posies - Dream All Day ~

A Seattle band, which many missed, but I recommend you discover. Not quite grunge, but not quite alternative, the song's simple riff with catchy lyrics and harmonies ensure you spend the next few days singing it. The psychedelic forest and foggiest day ever show the classic '90s style of videos with no pretension.

Curve - Superblaster *

I have considered the ravishing of guitar music by electronics a heavy sin for a long time. However, Curve can do it so easily, that I feel like it's the most natural thing in the world. The beating of a programmed pulse goes in absolute harmony with the sound of six strings and, together with dizzily dreamy vocals, it creates an expressively unified whole.

Tool - Sober +

A silent prayer and a loud confession. Promises and lies that just complicate everything. Corners of the mind, full of shadows of irreversible actions. They await in the darkness with commitments of highs and lows, mad happiness, and endless sorrow. A wild voyage with 'Tool' into the waters of alcohol and, at the same time, a desperate desire to return into the embrace of sobriety and stay within it.

Porno for Pyros - Pets   +

The bass line is recognisable even at the midnight hour and the singable chorus has the power of a child's nursery rhyme. Disappointment with the 'human race' heading towards its downfall is expressed with biting naivety. Maybe if Martians came and ruled over us, they would stop the spreading destruction and we people would become great pets. PfP in top form!

Mega City Four - Iron Sky   *

From time to time, an album gets literally stuck in my stereo and I can't get enough of it. In a miraculous interplay with my current mood, they merge into a perfect experience. 'Magic Bullets' was the soundtrack to one period of simple human happiness; although, it is not even a very cheery record. But 'to the happy, all is happy'.

Teenage Fanclub - Hang On   ~

This Scottish outfit rely only on their passion to play; they don't conform to any genre of music and can never be second guessed. Often cited as 'the world's best band', but mainly by other musicians, including Nirvana. The song not only gives a nod to Kurt at the beginning, but also takes you on a melancholy journey.

Boo-Yaa T.R.I.B.E. & Faith No More - Another Body Murdered *

Let an off-the-chain eccentric rock band and six huge Samoan rappers (who cannot be even chained) into a recording studio. Here is the result of an adrenaline experiment, in which Mike Patton proves how versatile a vocalist he is. And that gap between genius and madness is only a very fine line.

The Flaming Lips - Turn It On +

A simple and addictive melody, which rids you of the feeling that the easiness of being has long gone. Take off all of those dirty clothes, full of the layers and smells of everyday life, throw them into a washing machine, pour in an effective washing detergent branded Flaming Lips, and turn it on. The result will be a clean mind and perfect relaxation.

New Order - Regret *

The song thanks to which I discovered New Order. I have since listened to it another 999 times; yet, I have never grown tired of it. Maybe it is because of the jingly bassline, which you infallibly recognise after a few notes, and which distinguishes the band from millions of others. Or maybe it is the playful and a bit sentimental melody which will nest in your head. Or perhaps both?

Unrest - Cath Carroll *

A joyfully random video for a song about the singer Cath Carroll. I had no idea who she was, but now I yearn to know more about the woman who inspired such a song. A childlike cheerful confession of appreciation which will infect you with its playfulness and conjure up a smile on your face. Well, whoever can explain to me what this video is all about will be rewarded.

Candlebox - Cover Me ~

Every one of their song's lyrics makes you feel the melody was given to them by a higher power; they always fit so well together. This song is a complex building being constructed and as it gets higher so does the emotion within it. Vocals that make you want to cry, not with sadness, but with jealousy of his talent.

Type O Negative - Black No. 1 *

The moonshine soaks through the heavy clouds and reflects on a gravestone. The fog floats over the swamp and a werewolf howls in the distance. But it is somehow... melodic?! Welcome to the world of Type O Negative. At first sight, the perfect goth image, lengthy songs with bleak lyrics full of sadness and death, but, in the background, you can sense a sarcastic sneer.

Mindfunk - Goddess   +

A gem from the '90s that not many discovered. A hidden tree, which had its roots firmly imbedded in the hard-rock soil, full of nutrients rich on funk metal, grunge, and stoner rock moods. One of the peaks of their output is this song; besides the dense melody and torn lyrics, it will also amaze you with its unique emotive guitar solo.

Jamiroquai - Too Young to Die   ~

"Turn this rubbish off and put some real music on" my father always told me, until I played him this album. 'Real music' at its best. Jay Kay is a star vocalist, but so lost would he be without the sublime accompaniment of the group of musicians around him, who have no limits to the instruments used. Just listen.

Onyx - Slam   *

There are parties, and then there are parties you will remember. When the constellation of stars and people builds up an unrepeatable unity, no idea is too insane. To kill time, the testing of a flat's equipment is welcome, and nobody cares about the neighbours. Then it is time for bass boosted beats and a frenetic flow. Anything might happen but Onyx are the only ones you won't forget.

Björk - Venus As a Boy   ~

Iceland is famous for big, violent, and fiery eruptions, which helps explain why Björk is just like that too. This pint-sized woman delivers a punch to compete with the best boxers around, vocally of course. This bouncy and chilled song shows the diverseness she is now famous for, whilst still brilliant technically.

Archers of Loaf - Might   *

An intense ride on a rollercoaster, with cars dangerously charged with high voltage. You would even like to free yourself and get off, but it can't be done. So you are shaking in the busy captivity of guitars competing for the best discharge of screech, rattle, and feedback within one song. Whoever has experienced this just once got themselves a season ticket.

Suede - So Young   +

A cornerstone of Britpop – a London revelation – 'Suede' brought freshness and a subtle melodicism to the British music scene. Airy and bittersweet guitar pop completed by the characteristic vocals and wide range of the androgynous frontman Brett Anderson. You might wonder whether he reminds you of Jodie Foster a bit in this video? Just so you know, you are not the only one.

Nirvana - Heart-Shaped Box ×

Former punk simplicity is developed into new grounds with melodies more elaborate and complicated. Now, Nirvana's rebellion is already mainstream, the video is not furiously low budget anymore, it explodes with colours and swells with symbols. Kurt can share his innermost demons, wrapped in new musical ideas, in a much more intense way.

Life of Agony - This Time *

The singer does not care about technique. He sings vigorously and devotionally, no matter what the affection. The guitarist does not care about the purity of the genre. He builds monolithic compositions out of hard-core and metal riffs. The rhythm section does not care if you feel their punches in your stomach. They will not ease up for a moment. That is how Life of Agony sound. To not care about them would be a mistake.

Manic Street Preachers - From Despair to Where ~

The sort of song my neighbours could play loud at 4am and I would knock on their door, not to complain, but to join in. So powerful and precise, every riff is meaningfully played to induce feelings. My alarm clock should play this every morning, never would I mind being awake. Simply put, it makes me feel alive.

Leatherface - Do The Right Thing   *

I actually went to their gig by accident; however, I left it as a staunch fan. I immediately succumbed to their melodic punk rock, delivered convincingly and with spirit. They played nothing but hits to my ears and whoever manages to get used to Frankie Stubbs' hoarse voice can either love them ... or love them.

PJ Harvey - Man-size   +

A simple guitar riff which twines like a snake around the whole song and creates a musical mantra. The ability to arrange maximum effect in minimum space, where the lyrics are supporting pillars. The sarcasm is lightened by humour. Polly Jean is simply a quality writing investigative journalist, of her own soul. Of man-size.

Urge Overkill - Sister Havana   *

The biggest rock dudes. Only they know to what degree they really mean their retro image, and at what point they are poking fun at you. The writing on their foreheads says: "Chicks, monies, gears." Also, rock and roll till death, of course. They will break your heart, drink the whole bar dry, smoke all the cigars and you will still thank them. Because they are just that cool.

Living Colour - Nothingness *

I first heard 'Stain' when I left to live on the other side of the globe for nine months. It is really not much of a kind album, the beasts from Living Colour are gnarling and scratching more than ever before. However, the album also has their, perhaps, most moving song on it. A majestic statement describing exactly how I felt back then.

A Tribe Called Quest - Award Tour ~

This rap with rhyme, a perfect moment in time, with the bounce and the rhythm, just sat back, chillin'. Ain't listening to the lyrics coz they're too fast to know, gonna buy the CD and read the inside show. This band kicks it hard and it still ain't stopped, 'til I heard these, I just liked pop.

Morphine - Buena *

They did not choose their name accidentally, they are equally addictive. A two-string bass, a saxophone, drums, and a VOICE. With minimal presence of instruments, they were able to create an unbelievably strong, almost palpably thick, atmosphere. In a dangerous combination with the singer's bewitching baritone, their music has the ability to absorb me completely.

Paw - Jessie +

A criminally underrated band from Kansas. Aggressive riffs of individual verses are alternating with a catchy chorus backed by slide guitar. But do not be fooled, there is no barn dancing going on here. The smell of a white-hot lamp amp, kicking drums and the singer's rasp will not disappoint you if a rock heart beats in your chest.

Radiohead - Stop Whispering ~

Imagine a man in agony and pain, and then he starts to sing. The 'non-whispering' and tortured voice of Thom draws you into his world and ensures you feel his emotions entirely. The band's clever approach to writing enables you to hear his voice and not to notice the amazing accompaniment, which subtly resides.

Quicksand - Dine Alone *

Although they arose from the ashes of bands who played fast old school New York hardcore, Quicksand created their own unique sound. What they lacked in speed, they gained in huge metal shoed guitar riffs. The rhythm section rolls with the effectiveness of a bulldozer and the forcible, yet surprisingly melodic singing, will hit you right where you will feel it.

The Cranberries - Linger ~

With such a strong Irish brogue, it is easy to see why the band could be classed as alternative. But they combine beautiful lyrics with folk and rock support which helped put them on the map as simply The Cranberries. I am not a fan of cranberries, but these ones can be served with anything, and I will devour all day.

The God Machine - Home *

We come into this world in blood and tears and live our life with the knowledge that we were made from dust, and to dust we will return. So why should we live then? The God Machine turned the burden of all their doubts, anger, and pain into a monumental (double) debut album. The album is heavy, yet fragile and real at the same time. As is human life.

Green Apple Quick Step - Dirty Water Ocean +

A group from Seattle who cannot deny their home scene with the output. Their roots obviously didn't only get clean water, they strayed too close to the dirty ocean water. They do not want to, but they have to drink the germs of diseases, which change the velvety skin into a dead cow's leather. The bizarre lyrics are saved by swinging riffs and a fully rocking bass playerette.

Radiohead - Creep +

A hit loved by fans and eagerly awaited at concerts; yet, Radiohead removed this music child of theirs from setlists for a very long time. The overly personal message of the song might sometimes be a reliable trigger for old hurts and grievances. Still, those are also part of our life journeys and make us who we are today.

Stakka Bo - Here We Go *

Have you ever seen a hat shaped like a plant pot? How about a rapping Swede with a moustache? And a black ladybug? Because if you haven't, you can see that all now. Fortunately, after the first minute, you will no longer pay attention but choose to dance instead. That's because this frisky track has a beat with the potential to destroy a dance floor, and a chorus you will be singing for the whole week to come.

Paul Weller - Wild Wood ~

Stranded and lost alone, in the deep forest, trying to escape its clutches. The small bursts of controlled aggression in the song show the panic, whilst the soft cloud of repeating guitar strumming shows the perseverance within us all. Vocals that relax and calm you, but beware, they can affect you deeply.

Superchunk - Precision Auto *

After the explosion of the 'guitar nirvana' at the beginning of the '90s, Superchunk became a hot ticket for recording companies as another cash cow. But they showed them the finger with a smile and kept releasing their records on their own label. Therefore, the hyperactive opener of their third album remained a hit only for fans of the indie scene.

Ice-T - I Ain't New Ta This +

An original gangsta and an epic MC. He hates the L.A.P.D., sloppy verses, and artists who rip themselves off. However, he likes to count fat cash, slap that nicely shaped tanned ass, and stab the reporter who doesn't like him in the neck. His sleep is as deep as his lyrics. Nothing new for Ice-T. He is quite a nice guy. Just do not to piss him off.

Björk - Big Time Sensuality *

A freckly, jumping fidgeter, riding on the back of a truck around New York, has unmistakably attracted me by the changeable personality, charisma, and the primal sex appeal. Beautiful in her otherness, and without reins in her passion for music. Even though she created more adventurous and visually colourful videos, she made that first, important, impression on me with this one.

Aphex Twin - On   *

He already came clean in his ambient works about his inclination towards the disturbing details with which he later made his name. He builds a fragile composition from splashed drops of the swell, the sea foam and breeze, only to bang you on your noggin' with the hit of a jagged beat. Not even a diving suit with a brass helmet will protect you from it.

The Verve - Slide Away   ~

A beaut of a guitar track that barely even charted. Moreish bass that does not leave you wanting, and a plucky guitar teamed with the usual strummed rhythm of the Verve. Vocals which play with your mind, is he singing about you, or about himself? The video suits a '90s grunge band, but somehow still works here.

Girl Trouble - My Hometown   *

A guaranteed hot tip for all those eager to dance. For those who have not left their scruples at home, just put them behind the bar. The gallants on stage are dishing out straight rock'n'roll already, so just straighten your jacket, comb your hair, and take to the dance-floor with a storm. And they haven't even started to shake their hips yet! Elvis is watching it all from behind the curtain and humming contently.

Barkmarket - Whipping Boy   +

Do you ever feel like nothing can unsettle you anymore and that you have your inner peace well under control? That you have never had the feeling of when a band enters your head, wraps your neurons like erupting magma and lets you feel the magic of music psychosis? Everything is most intense the first time. Like this free fall under the supervision of the doctors from Barkmarket.

Cypress Hill - Insane in the Brain   ~

Take a breath, count to three; now your ass is trapped in the flow. No escape, no way out, your body is infused into the rhythm, and your brain is now in sync. To be stupid was to dislike, but I fought against, thinking I'd be individual. It became too much, and I realised I was the stupid one, pure hip with extra hop.

Band of Susans - Blind   *

He who ever doubted that three guitar players in a band makes sense should play 'Veil'. A fantastically compact and sophisticated album, where you can get lost in the labyrinth of riffs, melodic interplays, and feedback for hours. Then only to find an unexpected reward at its end, in the appearance of a captivating tune – 'Blind'.

Idaho - God's Green Earth   *

During the daily grind, chased by tasks and tempted by possibilities, we do not get a chance to follow how our lives run year after year. There is not even time to slow down and feel the power of a precious moment because we worry we might be missing something in the meantime. The ceremonially wistful music of Idaho has the power to soothe my flustered mind and put my feet back on the ground for a while.

Cosmic Psychos - Rain Gauge   *

If you like to drink beer, stare at boobs, drink beer, smack the moron at the next table in the mouth, drink beer, and listen to loud music, you will like them immediately. Farmers from the Australian outback who can, perhaps, do only one thing better than play their primal and noisy punk rock – shear sheep. Whoever doesn't like it will get mooned.

The Afghan Whigs - Gentlemen   +

Greg Dulli is a bard who is able to describe all the flavours of love. Also those parts which cause us to feel sick, be full of conflict and those actions which we would otherwise not even think of. We are burning in the furnace of passion, desire, and losing our mind. In spite of all that, we can rebound and remain gentlemen. Life is also about this. And so is this song.

Depeche Mode - I Feel You ×

Sometimes you take notice of a band because you hear about them everywhere, but you do not pay attention. But a breaking point might come and pull down the barrier of your disinterest. For me, it was their riff pumping the electrifying tension. When tension of a very different kind, provided by the fascinating Emmanuelle, joined in, DM had me in their pocket.

The Boo Radleys - Lazarus *

'Giant Steps' is a spectacular mosaic, which discloses another of its stones with each next listen. A masterfully elaborate album full of hidden details, sounds, noises, and melodic surprises. With its gentle verse and grandiose blast of brass instruments instead of a chorus, 'Lazarus' is an appropriate lure.

Swervedriver - Last Train to Satansville *

"Last train to Satansville is departing, take your seats. Hold your hats, we will stop only at the terminus. Maybe…" The unusual merging of guitar grandeur with surf rock inspiration suggestively rushes a lyrical drama to its conclusion. Sleepers are sweeping back in a galloping rhythm, the conductor is Chucky's dad, and there are wild dreams awaiting for nappers.

TAD - Leafy Incline   *

TAD weren't only called 'heavyweights from Seattle' because of the size of their singer's trousers. They played like they looked – their music was as uncompromising as their faces and their riffs as heavy as their frontman Tad. Fortune was afraid of them; thus, fame eluded them. But when they tried, they were able to write a purely melodic song. Like this one.

Blur - For Tomorrow   +

London. Arched verses and a catchy chorus pay tribute to its corners, atmosphere, and memories stored in particular places. The best view is said to be from Primrose Hill. The guys from Blur will give you a lift in a double-decker with the accompaniment of their music, to put you in its 'genius loci' with devotion and great emotion.

The Smashing Pumpkins - Disarm   ~

SP were able to make music to suit anybody's mood and with every song a different journey ensued. Bart Simpson said it best: "Making teenagers depressed is like shooting fish in a barrel". They were popular with teens because they 'got' that feeling. Suitable for the teens of today, and all of us teens from back then.

Dig - Believe *

We often find stuff when we are not looking for anything. Moreover, in a place entirely unlikely. One of my most favourite tunes of the '90s found me. A friend of mine stuck a CD into my hand and said: "Just play it." I was immediately captivated with the attack of three guitars and a clear slogan. Why don't I believe in my own God? I do indeed…

Belly - Gepetto *

If a group of rowdy kids run into your rehearsal space, you cannot tune your instruments very quickly. But when Belly start to play this song, you might be the one 'tuned' to a sing-song mood faster than you expected. And if you let yourself be carried away by its exultant guitar motif, you might as well jump for joy. Even if you were carved by Papa Geppetto.

Seaweed - Kid Candy *

There are bands which sell out arenas, others can just rule the charts. Seaweed are the kings of Friday nights in packed clubs. They do not shy away from anything and are happy with their few dirty chords, boosted amps and a hearty crowd under the stage. They will gladly pump out as much energy as anybody can take. They'll have some for you too.

Brad - 20th century   +

The group Brad comprises of members from bands like Pearl Jam, Malfunkshun, and Satchel, they created a spare room full of calmer and different styles as an alternative to the noisier garage of grunge. A slap bass, a repetitive guitar riff, and Shawn Smith's high-pitched vocals will guide you through the 20th century until its very end. And maybe even a little bit further.

Suede - Animal Nitrate   *

An invasion of pop from the British Isles left me cold from the beginning. (Yes.) I do not salivate over guitar solos; they tend to irritate me. (Yes.) At 1:45 comes the reason why solo guitarists should be taken into account. (Yes.) After Animal Nitrate, I started to give Britpop much greater respect. (Yes.) Suede. (Yes.)

Dunaj - Jednou   *

This band boldly, yet appropriately, chose their name after one of the great European rivers. The untamed stream of its music flows through picturesque nooks and dark crannies and hides unexpected vortexes as well as treacherous shallows. Trying to sail it is as much a challenge as it is a temptation. The risk of drowning is high but, in this case, it is welcome.

Slowdive - Alison   *

"I can take despair. It's the hope I can't stand."* Relationships are sometimes complicated, especially when it comes to a collision of feelings and the mind. Should I stay or should I go? Should I keep trying or should I give up? A beautiful song where you do not find a solution. But it is good to know that you are not the only one... And people say life is like licking honey off a thorn. So is love.

Les Thugs - As Happy As Possible   *

This simple video uncovers the exact roots of my own way of discovering and enjoying music – late night music shows, excitedly playing air drums, and jumping around the room. I used to jot down the bands I discovered which I just 'had to have'. If I had heard Les Thugs back then, I would have noted them down with an exclamation mark and a double underline.

Nudeswirl - F-Sharp   *

When I hear someone lamenting about how everything was better and nicer back then, it revs me up. But then I come across a record like this and I just say: "Why does no one play like this anymore?" Big rock guitars embroidered with feedback and a full bass sound supported with the firm hits of drums air my room out, I don't even have to open the window.

Red Hot Chili Peppers - Soul To Squeeze ~

This fun and freaky sideshow video seems harmless enough; it is only when you listen to the lyrics and let them overpower you that you see the truth. Through song, RHCP have not only struck a deep dark chord with many, but given hope to those who need it most. This squeezes out my soul through tears from my eyes.

Wu Tang Clan - C.R.E.A.M. *

A bold gang with an enterprising plan to conquer the music world. Their mission was successful – the creative businessmen of Wu-Tang Clan are often labelled as the best hip-hop band in the world. Their original productions and crew of distinctive rappers armed with an arsenal of precise verses and brilliant rhymes are the reason why.

Greta - Fathom *

The musical taste of the demented rockers Beavis & Butthead from the MTV cartoon show really wasn't for everyone. They often played surprisingly good songs by obscure bands, which were not to be seen anywhere else. They killed me with this curious example, with a furious riff, an unexpected guitar solo, a melodic chorus, and the singer wearing a dress.

Polvo - Tilebreaker   *

I have a theory that Polvo have a non-playing member in the band. He disturbs the others if they are all correctly playing the same song, or he detunes their instruments if the composition sounds too normal. The result is a sound adventure where you do not have a clue what could happen in the next second and you will discover the delight of disharmony.

The Reverend Horton Heat - Wiggle Stick   *

This reverend's sermons do not take place in church. A consecrated place would spontaneously burst into flames and break down into a pile of rubble after his entrance, in a self-defence attempt to preserve its purity. Therefore, he wanders from town to town and sows his sinful doctrine, vested in the robe of hot rockabilly, into curious ears found in rock clubs.

Lenny Kravitz - Are You Gonna Go My Way   ~

A slick, quick, and raw riff is all this song is, but nobody can listen to it and not have their pulse race at breakneck speed. Any party back in the day, had to have a pinnacle song of the evening, to which everybody would dance no matter what, and this song was always the lifting tool used, with great results.

Už jsme doma - Hollywood *

Tireless globetrotters and more of their homecomings. On their journeys, they look for a bone of contention rolled somewhere in the middle of words to beat the fragments of knowledge into verses and paint with vigorous strokes of the brush into sweaty scores. Intellectual punk or avant-garde symphony? Good ears are not enough, the willingness to listen is needed.

Dead Can Dance - The Carnival Is Over *

A brilliant picture interpretation of music, which is too ethereal and ungraspable to be from this world. Music that holds in itself the echoes of ancient tunes, deep internal feelings, but also hints of memories from the realm of Morpheus. Music that has the power to get you to look yourself in the eye with humility.

New Model Army - Here Comes the War *

Not even the greatest studio recording can overpower the music experience from the perfect gig. Whoever doesn't understand this should go and see New Model Army. I've seen and heard many sorts of things and now I do not have to be in every crowd. But when they started to play this one, the tension was just unbearable. I had to run into the pit and cry all the worldly woes out of me.

Soundgarden

The Offspring

Weezer

Oasis

Blur

Nick Cave & The Bad Seeds

Green Day

Method Man

Jeff Buckley

Therapy?

Hole

Nine Inch Nails

Portishead

Underworld

The Stone Roses

1994

It only took two years for alternative rock to make the rapid ascent from the garage to the centre of the spotlight. Its popularity peaked and, as it did, a pursuant question emerged asking what it actually was an alternative to now. With their work, its representatives initially resisted the status of rock stars, but soon they sold hundreds of thousands of records, made a name on the pages of leading music periodicals, were supported by MTV, and sold out arenas rather than clubs. Rebelling against the mainstream, they gradually became part of it. Two bands, which unintentionally found themselves in the centre of media attention, took a strong position on the situation. *Pearl Jam* tried to get off the bandwagon. They withdrew into seclusion, stopped giving interviews and shooting videos, and let only their music speak for them. *Nirvana*'s frontman Kurt Cobain did not see a way back. He confessed his feelings of frustration and burnout in the lines of his farewell letter and closed a chapter in music history by committing suicide. Although the music industry's merry-go-round did not stop for a moment, his departure prompted a redirection of its interests. The next genre change was far from stopping the echoes from the American independent scene, but voices from the other side of the ocean were already clamouring to have their say.

The beginning of the year in no way suggested the grunge story would be nearing its final act any time soon. On the contrary, some of its main characters were just reaching their creative peak. They broke away from what was expected of the genre and, in search of their own identity, unearthed some real gems.

Tired of endless touring and battling their personal demons, *Alice in Chains* booked a week of studio time in between two legs of their tour. Without a single pre-prepared composition or any ambition for the result of their efforts to be released, an eruption of spontaneous creativity ultimately resulted in the EP *Jar of Flies*. Seven chillingly beautiful, mostly acoustic songs met with rapturous reception as the record became the first ever mini-album to reach the top of the US album chart. *Soundgarden* worked on their new album for much longer, not leaving the studio for months. They experimented with the sound and the tuning of the instruments to the point of exhaustion to build the fascinating, seventy-minute *Superunknown* bit by bit. This tightly-wrapped monolith, which does not crumble into a shapeless pile of rubble even under the weight of demanding riffs and unpredictable rhythms, is decorated with unique melodies, shrouded in an aura of mystery, and the band deservedly received a multi-platinum award for it.

Stone Temple Pilots continued to struggle with the disfavour of music critics. However, many were silenced by their new release *Purple*, a powerful rock record on which they honed their signature sound and displayed their melodic instinct for admiration. With confidence, they brushed talk of similarities with other bands under the carpet. *Hole* and *Nirvana* were connected not only by the marriage of Courtney Love and Kurt Cobain, but also by a similar musical development. Following a furious punk rock debut, on their second studio album *Live Through This*, they worked with dynamics and pop influences in a much more sensitive way, i.e., the tried and tested recipe according to which *Nevermind* was also cooked. And they could easily be accused of plagiarism if the record was not so great it could stand its own ground.

Kurt Cobain's memory was honoured by MTV with repeated reruns of the *Nirvana* concert from the 'Unplugged' series. This popular format was launched at the end of 1989 and its essence was the live renderings of originally electric songs into acoustic form. The concept benefited from the intimate atmosphere of the performances on a small stage, which also allowed the audience to enjoy an almost authentic concert experience from their own living room. Some of the performers rehearsed their greatest hits for this occasion, others tried to bring a bit of refreshment to the effective, but, over time, rather monotonous concept.

The Cure left their typical gloomy mood in the rehearsal room; instead, they brought a bunch of unusual instruments, such as a xylophone, kazoo, bassoon and even a toy piano. The evening called 'Yo! Unplugged Rap' enlightened the uninitiated, proving the art of rap is not only based on beats, but works equally well in conjunction with classical instruments. *LL Cool J* took care of a primal, adrenaline-pumped, finale. *Pearl Jam* managed to keep their temper in check, that is, until an unexpected minor accident occurred. After that, they no longer had a reason to tame themselves and, in the wild ending, they completely forgot they were actually playing a peaceful acoustic set. *Stone Temple Pilots* reworked one of their own hits into a swing version and ended up enjoying their unplugged performance so much that an acoustic block became a regular part of their concerts in the years to come. *Nirvana* ditched the hits for a change. They reached for lesser-known songs, threw in a few popular cover versions for good measure, and lent the stage to their 'brothers', the *Meat Puppets*.

Björk prepared a breath-taking performance, and for many viewers, she not only completely reformatted the old idea of an unplugged performance but also music in general. Not all records from this successful series were released on physical media; thus, many of them acquired cult status in the days before the existence of the Internet. They became the subject of a frenzy and circulated among fans on worn-out videotapes.

Whether caused by the decision of the programme's producers or due to the rebellious attitude of the artists towards such a form of presentation, many parts of MTV Unplugged remained only at the level of fans' dreams. However, several performers who would have been perfect for such a performance, at least entered 1994 with great records.

The giant of country and folk *Johnny Cash* was not going to rest even after a career lasting more than three decades. On the contrary, he had just signed a contract with a label previously associated with hip-hop and heavy metal. In his own living room and only accompanied by his guitar, he recorded a warmly received album *American Recordings*, sparking a revival of interest in his work and brought it to a whole new audience. *Jeff Buckley* was still to find his fans; after months of playing solo in cafes and clubs, he put together a live band. On his debut album *Grace*, he finally immortalised his own original repertoire as well as some well-known covers. The album quickly earned him respect and recognition in music circles, even though it took some time for a wider audience to acquire the emotional depth of his songs and the piercing pitch of his voice. When *Morrissey* wrote his previous record with two new guitarists, he must have congratulated himself on how lucky he was in their selection. On their second joint work *Vauxhall and I*, they moved away from intense rock and political provocations towards deep songs, interwoven with personal themes. These not only enthused fans in their native England but also across the ocean, and their fruitful song-writing partnership was to last another fifteen years.

Even with their eighth effort, *Let Love In*, the antipodean *Nick Cave* and the inseparably linked *Bad Seeds* aimed nowhere else but directly into the heart. Despite the album's name, they avoided sentiment by far; after all, love can also be a bitch and has many forms. Purifying and punishing, uplifting and painfully sensual, fleeting, and unattainable, in the diabolical mind of the band's head and chief, it comes to life and dies in cinematically vivid images, transformed into verses.

Fans of alternative genres experienced an unusually ample musical harvest that year. A bag of notable recordings was torn open, and they were not hard to find, as they even penetrated mainstream airwaves, not to mention the daily supply of music videos from the MTV menu. The hunger for music filled with real emotions did not cease and its listeners often experienced bleak reckonings with the world or their own inner selves through the lyrics of the songs together with their authors.

Nine Inch Nails found more than enough food for thought on their new record. Their conceptual opus *The Downward Spiral*, fine-tuned to the last detail, tells a gloomy story of a person living on a slippery slope and his descent towards an inevitable end. It is a carefully composed industrial racket, in which bursts of aggressiveness from electronically crippled instruments are interspersed with fragile, seemingly peaceful nooks and crannies. Together, they form a musical image of the human mind plagued by advancing madness. While on their last two mega successful albums *R.E.M.* discovered the magic of the sound of acoustic instruments, they chose a really loud return to concert stages to present their new record. They named it *Monster* and covered it in layers of distorted guitar tones. However, during the process of recording, the burden of popularity as well as the deaths of several friends and family members fell on the band. Traces of the struggle with the pitfalls of mass favour of fans, loss of privacy, and sadness from the loss of their loved ones crept not only into the lyrics of the songs but also the gloomy mood of the band, reflected in the sound of the recording.

Weezer's eponymous debut brought a probe into the mental processes taking place behind the thick lenses of a shy introvert glasses. Feelings of misunderstanding, uncertainty, and loneliness are masked by loud mimicry of down-tuned guitars, yet catchy pop melodies bring them to the surface. Die-hard fans of alternative rock shook their heads in disapproval, but those who welcomed the album not only as a guilty pleasure but also as a pleasant diversion from the gloomy musical offer prevailed.

The heavy clouds on the radio airwaves were dispersed by fresh winds from sunny California. There, since the end of the 1980s, various forms of punk rock had been successfully infected with pop melodies. The local pop punk underground flourished, ploughed by bands giving concerts, stirred by the supervision of punk fanzines, and watered by a shower of recordings from independent labels. It was only a matter of time before this subculture found itself in the field of vision of talent scouts of big companies in search of a musical alternative.

They mainly put their hopes in *Bad Religion*, much appreciated by the scene, and their upcoming album *Stranger Than Fiction*, but there were two other dark horses on whose backs punk rock rushed into the sales and daily radio rotation charts. After two independent records, *Green Day* released their third effort on a major label. Driven by the power of their infectiously melodic songs and cheeky charm, *Dookie* was an absolute smash. The first single, *Longview*, caught on the radio, but the band finally broke through with a memorable performance at the Woodstock '94 festival. Millions of television viewers watched them mud fighting with their fans. In the course of the escalated finale, the singer mooned everyone and, in the final scrum right on stage, the bassist knocked out a few teeth after falling on the stage monitors. After such an advertisement, young people from all over the country nearly broke their legs running to buy the record and it literally disappeared from the shelves at lightning speed.

Only two months after *Green Day*, *The Offspring* also released their third album. Their noticeably harder, stormier, but no less melodious *Smash* came out on an independent label. The single *Come Out and Play* was to prepare the ground for it. The catchy slogan in the chorus and the unusual, oriental, guitar riff worked in a way that no one expected. The song was made into a radio hit and the album one of the musical sensations of the year, which at the time of its release set the record for the best-selling independent record ever and sold more than ten million copies worldwide. Nothing could stop the punk rock avalanche now.

The independent punk label 'Epitaph' had a serious stake in its launch and its powerful impact in the subsequent years. It was founded in 1981 by Brett Gurewitz, the guitarist and half of the songwriting tandem of *Bad Religion*. At first, it was just a publishing house for his band, but it did not just end there. He put the promisingly developing label on the backburner to attend recording school only to open the 'Westbeach Recorders' studio upon completion, where several records for bands that became heroes of the Californian punk rock were later produced.

The Epitaph catalogue began its enhancement at the end of the '80s. It was gradually to add to its roster the ultra-fast jokers *NOFX*, the positive motivators *Pennywise*, the inconspicuous hard workers *Down By Law*, and the street scoundrels *Rancid*, all swearing by straight-forward, melody-filled punk rock. *Bad Religion*, who, at the turn of the decade, stubbornly released only excellent and even better records, were at the forefront. The scene quickly gained popularity, which was also helped by an affinity with the skate community. It manifested itself in the abundant use of punk music not only during skateboarding or surfing events, but especially in their promotional videos. At the beginning of the '90s, Epitaph was already able to process orders for a million records from its catalogue, annually.

But not even that could have prepared the label for the events of 1994, when *The Offspring* made it famous. The overwhelming success of their album *Smash* brought with it astronomical offers from major labels to collaborate on its distribution. However, Brett Gurewitz decided to resist them all and keep the label independent. He mortgaged his house, left *Bad Religion*, and plunged into a risky venture – to take care of a global bestseller on his own. His audacity paid off.

Epitaph survived, continued to prosper and, over time, enriched its musical scope with related genres. Equally warmly, it welcomed *Gas Huffer*, who played garage punk, *Voodoo Glow Skulls*, who mixed punk with bouncy ska, and old school hardcore legends *Agnostic Front* in order to build an indestructible monument to dirty chords and choir chants. As long as the label exists, punk will definitely not die.

A punk approach to creative work does not necessarily have to lead to the production of punk. The desire to do things their own way, albeit often on their uppers and using cheaply available equipment, has given birth to a great number of unique bands in the musical underground since the early '80s. Their album attempts, recorded in garages or bedrooms on their own four-track tape recorders, significantly influenced the face of independent rock and, due to their questionable sound quality, earned the label 'lo-fi'. Various technical imperfections or the hissing of a reused tape became an organic part of their sound. They emphasised the charm of spontaneous creativity and, as a result, were not only tolerated but, in many cases, even became an irreplaceable ingredient of their work.

Guided By Voices are a collective of randomly occurring members rather than a regular band, and this element of unpredictability is captured on their breakthrough album *Bee Thousand*. This collection of quicky-put-together home recordings as well as fully fledged songs, rarely more than two minutes in duration, sounds like a demo at best. However, the compositional skill and the ease with which influences of pop, psychedelic rock, and punk intertwine on the album make it a masterpiece. After a series of chaotic self-recorded records, *Sebadoh* also explored the possibilities of organised studio work. While their older work often gave the impression of wild compilations, their new album *Bakesale*, on the contrary, held together perfectly. Cleaned from the deposit of sonic anarchy and unbridled experiments, it is the band's most accessible work and a showcase of pure indie rock songwriting.

176

In the first years of their existence, *Pavement* also had a chance to go crazy by burying their songs in ear-splitting guitar screeching and the distorting noise of cheap studios. Although on their second album *Crooked Rain, Crooked Rain* they paid more attention to its sound, this did not take away from the clever lunacy that is inherent in their songs.

The independent comedy *Clerks* (1994) provided remarkable proof that it is possible to create not only an album but also a feature-length film with nationwide distribution with minimum funds – with receipts of over three million, it cost an unbelievable 27,575 dollars to shoot. However, it is also one of those few films whose costs for settling licensing rights to the music used exceeded the shooting budget itself. The soundtrack to the film offers a cross-section of the universe of alternative rock. The flag bearers of the punk rock scene, *Bad Religion*, met here with underground favourites *Girls Against Boys* and *The Jesus Lizard*; *Corrosion of Conformity* contributed with a bit of metal, and *Alice in Chains* threw in a semi-acoustic ballad. The accompanying music video with a paraphrase of one of the key scenes from the film was provided by *Soul Asylum*. Although they neither played instruments nor sang, they demonstrated their courage, personal pressure, and fearlessness in scraps.

Music also played a significant role in the success of the film adaptation of the comic book *The Crow* (1994). The dark artwork itself drew inspiration for its range of dark emotions from the music and lyrics of *Joy Division* and *The Cure*. The filmmakers faithfully managed to transfer it to the screen and use songs that colour the events in the story to create a soundtrack that tempts the imagination, darker than the night and denser than tar. *The Cure* could not be left out, as no one else could better create a feeling of creeping restlessness. *Nine Inch Nails* possess the viewers with an exigent remake of a *Joy Division* song, *Rollins Band* delivers a cruel rock beating, *The Jesus and Mary Chain* captures the sleepy atmosphere of a god-forsaken bar just before last call, the romantic *Medicine* caresses the soul, and

Pantera shines with a ferocious metal whirlwind. Together, they form a balanced amalgam of gothic, industrial, and alternative rock, which will stand up not only as a marketing tool to promote the film but, first and foremost, as a cohesive work, which functions perfectly even without any knowledge of it.

In the turbulent first half of the '90s, diverse sound forms surfaced in rapid succession during the alternating genre waves. Even your ordinary listener was exposed to music they would otherwise probably not have stumbled upon and, thus, could expand the ranks of its fans. The short-lived appearance of such bands as *Metallica*, *Megadeth*, or *Pantera* in commercial waters helped increase the popularity of heavy rock genres, as well as the emergence of new offshoots with the potential to appeal not only to orthodox metal hordes.

On their debut record *Burn My Eyes*, *Machine Head* mixed brutal riffs and concentrated anger into a hearty serving of textbook 'groove metal'. The inexorable rolling of a running bulldozer, which tries to crush the listener to a pulp while fully conscious, was emphasised by sporadic steps towards the breakneck tempos of thrash metal. They immediately set out to test their material on a tour thanks to which, after a series of concerts in the company of worthy thrashers *Slayer*, they built a devoted fan base in Europe. After more than a year of delays caused by changes in the ownership of their record company, *Kyuss* released a colossal eponymous album, also known, thanks to its cover photo, as *Welcome to Sky Valley*. The music on it admirably manages to encompass the vastness of the arid desert plains in which their hometown lies and weighs as much as the skies above. Thanks to a guitar attack with the intensity of a hurricane and trips into psychedelic corners, *Kyuss* lay the fundaments for the sound of the 'stoner rock' scene that was to come later.

Korn did not worry too much when naming their first album either; they, however, fundamentally marked the face of metal music for the next few years. Their aggressively charged compositions without a single guitar solo, an interplay of chopped-off guitar riffs, hip-hop rhythms, and brain-piercing vocals moving from ominous whispers to psychotic roars without any warning became the prototype of the new form called 'nu metal'. It was soon to take the position of one of the most striking, as well as the most controversial, metal genres.

Meanwhile, in the hip-hop field, a charged battle between East Coast and West Coast rappers was heating up. After several years of western dominance, the centre of gravity of hip-hop events shifted back to its cradle and centre of the East Coast, New York. The scene there stood out for its emphasis on artfully written lyrics, complexly structured rhymes, and the skilful use of language means. All these strengths shone through in a series of recordings that emerged from it in 1994.

Nas recorded what is now a classic work of the scene; words of praise and analysis of his debut *Illmatic* have since been written on stacks of paper. He introduced himself on it as a narrator of absorbing stories from his hometown, built from complex but comprehensible verses. Through them, the listener is drawn into a panopticon of scenes from the street, enlivened by colourful descriptions of life and populated by local characters. This provides the listener with an almost tangible experience; his back is covered exclusively by the production elite. Even *DJ Premier* provided some of his famous beats for this hip-hop masterpiece. However, this did not make him short change his own project *Gang Starr*, with whom, on their fourth studio album *Hard to Earn*, decided to put an end to the reputation of intellectual 'jazz-rap'. His partner on the mic, *Guru*, put good manners aside and spiced up his witty social commentary with coarser language, while *Primo* worked his magic with a wide variety of samples, proving that his strength is uniqueness rather than just one brilliantly mastered trick.

RZA, another ace producer and the mastermind behind *Wu-Tang Clan*, did not have anything to be ashamed of either. He started the second phase of their operation aimed at dominating the rap game with *Method Man*'s eponymous solo album, with *RZA* entirely taking care of the music side of this release. Like the home band's debut, *Tical* is a claustrophobic, dangerously dense mass of dark beats, made special by kung fu movie samples. *Method Man* works his way through it with undisguised enjoyment, delivering, between puffs, well-aimed blows with his rhymes in all directions.

The English port of Bristol not only served historically as a centre of trade with the British colonies, but also as a gateway to the country for immigrants from all over the world. Together with them, diverse cultural and music influences flowed into the city and intermingled in it.

The strong Caribbean community brought from its birthplace the tradition of 'soundsystems', a DJ grouping, which, with a crate of records and a pair of powerful speakers, unleashed fun not only in dance clubs but also from the bonnet of a car and right on the street. At first, they mainly played home genres like 'ska', 'dub', and especially 'reggae', but with the arrival of the '80s they also liked the increasingly widespread hip-hop, which equally respected and developed the work with the gramophone and vinyl records. Together with it, the soundsystem cocktail soaked in the scent of soul and R&B, as well as the art of rap and sampling. It was to be expected that it would not stop at playing records eclectically and that this wild bunch of genres would one day mature into a music form in its own right.

Thus, when one of the sophisticated soundsystems started its own work under the name *Massive Attack*, it did not have to look for inspiration for its sound for a long time. On their second record, *Protection*, released in 1994, they effortlessly fused the lilting rhythms of reggae, sample fragments, and hypnotic beats with elements of electronic music, while the instinctive flow of their half-rapped, half-declaimed lyrics was softened by velvety vocals. *Portishead*, who debuted in the same year, could also rely on an exceptional singer; yet they also could not deny their hip-hop roots. Although their album *Dummy* did without a single rapped verse, they densely layered their stealthily stepping beats with nerve-wracking scratching. Artfully selected samples lent the record the insistent drama of film music. An essential sound component of both bands was slow tempos, as well as a mysterious, sensual, aura surrounding their compositions. It was this evocative mood that gave birth to the genre label 'trip-hop', even though the bands themselves fought this term tooth and nail.

The British electronic scene with its clandestine dance parties and free-entry festivals for thousands of fun-seeking visitors had inevitably become a thorn in the side of law enforcement. At the end of the year, they submitted a bill to parliament, increasing the penalties for participants and organisers of such events. Paradoxically, in the same year, for the very first time in the history of the prestigious Glastonbury festival, the electronic duo *Orbital* presented itself as one of the main stars. Surrounded by a wall of machines, without a live guitar or at even a bass, they brought an enthusiastic crowd of forty thousand to the boil. Their triumphant concert made it officially clear that electronic music does not only belong in clubs but should also be reckoned with on the biggest stages. This fact was underlined by a few excellent studio recordings released that year.

On their *Dubnobasswithmyheadman* record, the reborn and musically completely rebooted *Underworld* combined the practices of old-world musicianship with the melodic beats of progressive house and 'techno', breathing life and the human spirit into mechanical rhythms. *The Future Sound of London* focused on completely different spheres of perception. The majestically flowing music of their double album *Lifeforms* spills into boundless ambient surfaces and sound textures, from which fragments of beats, melodies, and abstract rumblings randomly emerge. The hyperactive *Prodigy*, on the other hand, never abounded in subtlety and presented the listeners with an intense, sample-rich breakbeat splash of *Music for the Jilted*

Generation. With a combination of inventive aggressiveness and hellish charisma, they won over fans and climbed to the top of the album chart.

And so it happened that, although the trifling law finally came into effect in November, it could not seriously harm this music with 're-petitive beats'. In any case, it already occupied the top rungs of the music charts and was aiming not only for the daily rotation of radios but also the screens of music TV stations.

The wave of acceptance for electronic and newer musical styles was also reflected in the rise to prominence of Britpop. It respond-ed to the heavy hand of the American influence of grunge and the neo-psychedelia of the domestic Shoegaze scene. Britpop unapolo-getically borrowed from hits of the past to create a nostalgia-fuelled feeling of national positivity that had been missing in British life. An emphasis on local identity was prevalent, with acts becoming an extension of the regions which they inhabited. It would be driven by a ferocious duel fought between its two primary protagonists, rekindling old rivalries between the traditionally working-class North and the more well-heeled South.

The swagger and bravado emanating from the Gallagher brothers saw the beginning of *Oasis'* fiery affair with the music world, resulting in turbulence with the media, rival bands, and most of all each other. Their debut *Definitely Maybe* did not try to revolutionise, instead tak-ing Rock 'n' Roll fundamentals crafted by their idols and mastering them, creating a fresh yet familiar sound lingering between straight-forward, but catchy, lyrics and roaring guitars. If *Oasis* were the un-stoppable force, then *Blur* was the immovable object. They hit their stride with *Parklife*, a kaleidoscope of British life which itself would come to represent a huge part in a major cultural shift. A melting pot of contrasting influences, the record cast a wide net over the many sub-cultures of society while retaining a coherent style and tone. Its bouncy pop anthems with a taste of abstract experimentation, were permeated by a consistently light-hearted demeanour, just teetering on the edge of parody or sarcasm.

Although somewhat veterans at this stage, having released their first EP back in 1983, *Pulp* made their official entrance with *His 'n' Hers*, their first release on a major label. The record introduced the witty, conversational cadence of Jarvis Cocker, featuring overtly sexual narratives hiding behind playful guitar riffs.

Britpop revived awareness of guitar music from the British Isles, but its key players were far from the only ones pleasing the ears of Rock fans. There was an abundance of bands who were difficult to place in one bucket but were nonetheless breaking new ground in the genre.

The Stone Roses released a long-awaited follow-up to their eponymous album five and half years prior, in addition to a four-year absence from touring. The title *Second Coming* clearly alluded to a resurrection of sorts, hoping to rise from the ashes in a much-changed commercial environment, where Madchester was breathing its last with Britpop now monopolizing the attention of the British public. Although it did not inspire any lasting revival, the jam session feeling that the colourful, thumping beats create, allows the album to stand on its own two feet. "Post-Grunge" outfit *Bush* hit the ground running with debut *Sixteen Stone*, using the blueprints of Nirvana and Pearl Jam and building on that foundation. Its booming vocals paired with razor-sharp guitar riffs resonated loudly Stateside. Although finding a more lukewarm reception on home shores, they achieved the goal many British heavyweights had failed to do - to 'break America' - on their maiden voyage.

Alternative metal band *Therapy?* made a big step forward from their unpolished early releases with *Troublegum*, later rated as the Top Album of 1994 in the 1000th issue of Kerrang! magazine. Powerful melodies featured strongly at a time where simply being louder was en vogue, showing their resilience to adapt in a genre that was being redefined on a weekly basis. Celtic rockers *The Cranberries* picked up where their debut left off with the well-received *No Need to Argue*. While stylistically retaining the ethereal and dream-like feel of their previous outing, they took on a slightly heavier tone, both audibly and in lyrical content. It would see the beginning of the band's growing political stance, in some cases positing an accusatory tone directly at the listener.

There was a lot of interesting music happening on European shores, but the 11th annual MTV Video Music Awards captured little of it. The most notable import from Europe was *Björk*, with six nominations for the video *Human Behavior*, although, in the end, she left the award ceremony empty-handed.

In contrast, *R.E.M.* took home the most statuettes for the video for the song *Everybody Hurts*. While accepting the award for best director, their speech was sabotaged by the mysterious Nathanial Hörnblowér, protesting that director Spike Jonze had not won the award for his work with *Beastie Boys*. The band themselves coped with the disappointment in the best way possible; they played an adequately ferocious version of *Sabotage*, including a 'warm' message to the awards panel at the end. *The Smashing Pumpkins* also vented their frustration on stage for completely different reasons – the producers of the evening did not allow them to play a song other than *Disarm*. Their singer Billy Corgan rewarded them for this by butchering one of his most beautiful songs with aggressive vocals and violent guitar playing. Scott Weiland, the frontman of *Stone Temple Pilots*, already gave the impression that he was losing ground during the interview before the show. However, his performance on stage was not marked by this. In an unplugged fashion, he flawlessly sang their non-single *Pretty Penny*, and no one could have guessed what a painful path he was already walking.

Kurt Cobain, unfortunately, already knew what was at the other end. He tragically ended his life's journey just a few months before he and *Nirvana* were to accept the award for best alternative video for the song *Heart Shaped Box*. His bandmates and the audience in the hall honoured his memory with a short clip of archival and concert footage. *Snoop Doggy Dogg*, on the contrary, only impressively staged the scene from his own funeral. With the arrival of the second verse of *Murder Was the Case*, he emerged from behind the scenes and, backed by a gospel choir, finished the song in front of the audience. *Green Day* kept the song selection to the moment's inspiration and surprised their fans with the new piece *Armatage Shanks*. Another whole year passed before its studio version came out.

The target group of the MTV Video Music Awards was mainly the American audience, and the selection of the performers as well as the nominated videos corresponded to this. Naturally, it was dominated by domestic artists, while trends from overseas only received more attention once they built a certain following on American soil. Still, viewers on the old continent could watch live music events by means of videos broadcast by MTV Europe. The establishment of the annual MTV Europe Music Awards gala was, therefore, a logical step for European audiences to enjoy their favourites, while a generous space for artists from across the ocean was still available.

Its first year was held in 1994. The main difference in comparison to the American version of the programme was that, with the exception of the song of the year and the award for direction, it was not the videos that were nominated in the individual categories, but the artists. Another obvious difference was the panel's lack of acceptance of artists from niche genres. Even though the nominees included a whole host of new names from the alternative scene, the awards went to those who had the potential to cross over into the mainstream. A fan of musical otherness was perhaps only elevated when *The Prodigy* was honoured as the best dance group or when Mark Pellington was declared the best director thanks to the crazy *Hobo Humpin' Slobo Babe* video, which he made for the even crazier *Whale*.

Compared to their American colleagues, the programme makers of the evening did not summon much more courage either and relied on proven and safe pop, only broken by a scenographically imaginative performance by *Björk*. Dressed in an impressive outfit, slightly impractical for dancing, she performed a remixed version of *Big Time Sensuality* with *Fluke* providing electronic support. *Therapy?* played a completely different card when, without any decorations or stage props, they spluttered out *Die Laughing* at the audience. An honest mouthful of rock riffs was enhanced by a guest cellist and the traditionally determined performance of the drummer, who quite clearly drenched with sweat the last thread of his well-fitting suit.

The unmissable video for *Björk*'s *Human Behavior* was shot by the French director Michel Gondry. She scouted him based on his work for the band *Oui Oui*, in which he sat not only in the director's but also the drummer's chair. In these videos, he abundantly used elements of animation, camera tricks, and image manipulation, necessary to capture the flow of unrestrained fantasy so typical of his work. In it, visual gluttony is combined with attention to detail and a peculiar sense of humour goes hand in hand with an unsettling atmosphere.

This successful cooperation with *Björk* was not the only one; over the years, he made several more videos for her. His services were also used by *Inspiral Carpets*, *Black Crowes*, *Foo Fighters*, and *Beck*. They allowed him to drag them into a world where the fifth dimension is a common part of reality, the laws of physics have undergone drastic bullying, and the bogeyman's scarier brother lurks under the bed. He proved he was also able to slow down and let the mood of the song stand out in his work for *Massive Attack* and *Cibo Matto*, and he created crazy choreography for the dancey *Chemical Brothers* and *Daft Punk*. Although, while working with musicians, he did not waste offers from the advertising industry either. He made shorts for such brands as Nike, Levi's, GAP, and an especially memorable campaign for Smirnoff. In it, he used a visual effect that was later bought from him and perfected by the creators of the film *Matrix* (1999), now known as 'bullet time'.

He did not bow his head to the challenge of a feature film either. His second attempt, *Eternal Sunshine of the Spotless Mind* (2004), attracted positive reviews and won him an Oscar; this time, not as a director but as a co-writer of the screenplay. Jim Carrey and Kate Winslet shone in it as actors, while Michel Gondry gave the film a specific character with forays into surrealist sequences. He took a more traditional approach when documenting the spectacular hip-hop happening in *Dave Chappelle's Block Party* (2005). The source of his creativity has not dried up since then. He continues to create in the field of film, documentary, and, fortunately, he is still happy to find time for music videos.

The following pages feature video clips shot in support of singles released in 1994.

Selected and commented on by:
~ Shezz, + Zebra, * Rasťo, ‡ Veni, × Kubsson, « Julian

The Cranberries - Ridiculous Thoughts ‡

The story of a boy who finally got to hear the beautiful sound he had been longing for – the rock sound of the British Isles, in its simple melodic form. The Cranberries subdued the ears and hearts of the listeners with music exactly like this – straightforward, yet, still interesting enough to have a good reason to come back to it years later.

Rollins Band - Liar ~

Love it or hate it or just confused by it, either way, you have to respect it. The pure devilness of Henry's character is so good, it asks the question, is it actually a character? Would you be foolish enough to forgive him time and again, or be brave enough not to. Pure class, before class had even been defined.

Sebadoh - Rebound *

The greatest hit from an album without any duff tracks. With a basic instrument cast, and with zero studio magic. There is not even a guitar solo in sight! Just honest songs, with the impact of a solar plexus punch, and ingenious observations about the troubles of human relationships. A perfectly flawless album which influenced my music taste noticeably.

Stone Temple Pilots - Interstate Love Song +

If your girlfriend casually asks you if you are using and you deny it, even though you have just recorded a whole album continuously high on heroin, it really is an ugly lie. You wouldn't see the girlfriend for dust; however, a solid theme for a song about deceit in love will remain. The grungy STP are in an ardent embrace with melancholic country psychedelia.

Edwyn Collins - A Girl Like You ~

Luckily, this song didn't rely on a good video for it to become a hit. It had a certain 'class' to it which made it stand out. When it plays, I always feel it has a certain aroma which makes everybody loosen up and become friendlier and more approachable. It has certainly helped me more than a few times on nights out.

Frank Black - Headache ‡

Frank wrote this song back when he was fifteen, maybe that is why the video is so metaphorical. A simple unobtrusive melody and a rhythm in the vein of Pixies, the band from whose ashes this songwriter arose. With an appropriately high volume, it can lift you up every morning, except for the cases when you actually have a headache.

Terrorvision - Oblivion ~

Do not be oblivious to the obvious brilliance which is buried beneath this hard cheesy crust. Just because the band clearly contains nuts doesn't mean you should be allergic to them. With their tongues firmly pressed against cheeks, this not so serious song typifies this sprightly band thoroughly and entirely.

Sunny Day Real Estate - Seven *

The word 'Emo' was not always an insult which was associated with poseur bands and strange fashion. SDRE were one of the first to be labelled this because of their emotional vocals and unrestrained music served with passion. No fringes, black rags, or suicidal moods, just a unique tension, dynamics, and a chunk of believable feelings.

dEUS - Suds & Soda +

An explosive mix of psychedelia and ecstatic cheer of the fact that Friday had come. An adored anthem that I welcomed my guests with to weekend underground parties in the second half of the '90s. The room was carved with sharp tones of violin loops, throats resounded 'Friday' in unison and the outside world stopped and listened for a moment. dEUS ex clubroom!

Warren G feat. Nate Dogg - Regulate +

213. The telephone area code of Los Angeles and the name of the first band in which he wore down the microphone. A talented rapper with a love for music, sampled the first four bars of a funk song from the '80s and embedded a tense story from Long Beach into it. Hypnotising vocals provided by his mate Nate Dogg, and suddenly it was clear just who rules here.

Body Count - Necessary Evil ‡

People are not good; they just get used to each other. They at least try to stifle a necessary evil. 'Body Count' is a detergent for your brain. It rips it out of your head, washes it, then puts back again and you feel fresh and relaxed. Heavy metal and rap is the right cocktail for your mental health. Recommended by four out of five psychiatrists.

Pearl Jam - Not for You ~

Set in the 'no video' years, this is one of many that should have been included, but with the magic of the 20 year celebration, more joy for us. Lingering guitars that helped me sleep, alone or otherwise, holds memories of darkened nights walking from train stations with a portable CD player, pressing play every hour.

Velocity Girl - Sorry Again   *

We are who we are. We can change something about ourselves if we really want it. However, we do often try to make changes because of others; all that remains in the end is a sad "I am sorry." This is about that bitter break-up pill, coated in luscious icing made of girly vocals and gleeful guitars. Singable and sympathetic, such is the whole album "Simpatico!".

Jeff Buckley - Grace   +

We are given to the grace of our own mortality. Sometimes we do not mind our own dispensability. Other times we perceive it as essential and we are asking if we are ready to leave without fear. It is somehow smaller though if we walk through life with somebody at our side. It is, however, just waiting in the fire all along. Jeff is already out of these flames. Yet his music still burns.

The Wannadies - You and Me Song   *

The author of this happy pill must have shone like a Christmas tree in that particular moment. I don't know what I like more, the unusual combination of bossa nova and power pop, the cute but not kitschy lyrics, or the anthemically unforgettable chorus. Whoever doesn't feel like kissing or cuddling when listening to this might have a heart of stone.

Bush - Machinehead ‡

Breath in, breath out. Speedy guitars for a fast life. This is genuine brisk grunge. An ecstatic song about machines in our heads which push us forward and do not want to cease. We cannot stop them while we are alive, if someone else doesn't turn them off. Warning: After listening to this, you will want to do something and the tips of your fingers will itch.

Portishead - Glory Box ~

Those hidden desires that must not speak take hold of you and compel you to give in. A mistake you may regret, or a mistake worth making is always the choice to be made. Will you succumb to the temptations that lay before you or can you be strong and let lust pass you by? Three and a half minutes of pure naughtiness.

Autechre - Basscadet (Bcdtmx) *

What runs through the mind of your computer when you think it is in sleep mode? Maybe its processor is busy composing a befitting beat to another layer of a digital drone, bit after bit, calculating and coupling tiny glitches, whilst purring melodies from the depths of cybernetic space in its memory. Try to discreetly put your ear to it.

Nick Cave and The Bad Seeds - Do You Love Me? +

You would only in vain search for it on the beach on a sunny day. This kind of love twinkles in the shadows of night lamps and streets that smell of lust and sear with unfulfilled desires. It can enslave the mind and torture the body. It burns all disbelieves, until the end. Cave's created a cocktail of fatal love which would be a sin not to drink, in spite of its bitter taste.

Alice In Chains - No Excuses ~

This could almost be described as a soft, duet ballad, but then AIC can never quite be described accurately, as no words exist for the stupendously large amount of talent they had. The drumming on this takes my breath away with each listen, so much in fact I forget there are lyrics and other instruments to discover.

Primal Scream - Jailbird ‡

They have cruised the open sea of British rock for a while; for some time, they even strayed into quite a dancy Harbour. On this record, they were blown into waters reminiscent of the '60s. It can be heard, seen, and felt from their expression. If I wanted a band for my birthday party, I would call Primal Scream for sure. All would be happy and perfectly blustered.

The Stone Roses - Love Spreads   ~

Revolutionary, groundbreaking, and inspiring to the many bands who copied and followed them. Sometimes you don't know how good something is until it's gone. I only discovered their brilliance when they were apart, I became one of the many fans who prayed they would reform; now our prayers have briefly been answered.

Sick Of It All - Step Down   *

Fear often springs from a lack of knowledge and a reluctance to try to understand. Whoever has ever attempted to explain to their parents why they go to those violent, noisy, and threatening hardcore gigs, perhaps knows what I am talking about. Fortunately, there is an investigative reporter Sandal Weisberger and his fair report merges with an instructional video. Dads, watch this.

Stiltskin - Footsteps   +

Have you ever played the role of somebody's plaster for their pain who you trusted loved you? Could you just helplessly watch as you were erased and replaced? Were you left on the edge between rediscovering the meaning of life and a docile feeling of fading out forever? If you have been through something like this, just consider listening to this song. It may open old wounds.

Beck - Loser +

The worst flow of a white pseudo-rapper or one of the most genius efforts of a desperate beginner? The former does not negate the latter. A surrealistic-psychedelic kaleidoscope of existential misery was able to amaze so many people that, even today, it seems like bad luck is the best thing that can stick to a musician's heels.

Suede - We Are The Pigs ‡

Glam rock dressed in a marzipan of curvy shapes with lemon glazing? The guitar parts as juicy as a punch cake? This is Suede, a sweet and sour dessert from the British rock confectionery. Every tone has its meaning, every melody unwraps and closes. Their endeavour for unmindful impeccability is imposing. The London of the '90s is not coming back, unfortunately.

Soundgarden - Fell On Black Days ~

Not quite perfection but damn close. When rock is not enough, when Grunge seems too old school and when you need to fill that gap, here is the killer filler. Never can it be said that SG have sold out. This example shows the basic formula of success – four real musicians with passion for what they do – will never fail.

Supersuckers - Creepy Jackalope Eye   *

"This album is dedicated to the good fuckers, and those who want to be good fuckers!" A record starting with such a manifesto cannot disappoint. An exemplary piece, by the masters of stable-like punk rock, with the speed of a stud-horse mustang and the spirit of a crowded bar. Cowboy hats, odd jokes, and the smell of horse dung. Enough fun to piss your pants.

Sponge - Plowed   +

'Plowed' has an affect on me like a proper shot of quality gin. The blood in my veins starts to boil and my temples pulse with the weight of the whole world's pulsating. For a moment, I recall the times of youth and impetuosity. When I emerge back to reality after the song ends, I am grateful in the fact that it always reminds me how it felt to be ploughed in music.

The Prodigy - Voodoo People   *

This literally glued me to the screen. I didn't care that "I don't listen to dance music", I didn't even realise they had recreated the riff from my favourite Nirvana song. The ecstatic rhythm rolled me over like an avalanche, and I just stared disbelievengly at what was happening before my eyes. One of those moments when I realised genres do not matter.

Therapy? - Screamager ‡

Therapy? start where other rock bands end. They try to take punk-rock to its excellence. Andy Cairns' voice sounds obstinate – one moment gentle as a caress, the next sharp as a razor. But it will not put you to sleep, nor will it cut you. If you want some peace to rest, tune into something on the radio. If you like to relax to hard music, press Play.

Green Day - When I Come Around ~

Walk down your street and see the many different kinds of people. All different in looks, wealth, and intelligence, but with all the same worries, fears, and yearning to be accepted. Great video showing how lives intertwine and remind us that every one of us is an individual, it's the one thing we all have in common.

Massive Attack - Karmacoma *

An anxious video entering the area of a feverish dream, where the imagination gets out of control and its relentlessly restful steps are heading towards a nightmare. Rooms of the hotel where you would not want to spend the night uncover their secrets and an obsessive beat underscores a thickening atmosphere in a strained expectation of the story's climax.

Hex - 1,2,3, dobrý deň   +

Hardly any Slovak band managed to give a concert in the USA. 'Hex' enjoyed their performance at SXSW in Austin. John Peel from BBC Radio liked them so much, he invited them on his show. The guys declined, they chose to go for a beer in their favourite pub instead. John Peel must have been disappointed. That's why I mainly dedicate this song to his memory.

R.E.M. - What's the Frequency, Kenneth?   ~

A wonderfully safe pop-rock song by the otherwise band of trend-setters that actually became a fan favourite. The video and Mr. Stipe's aggressive dancing seem to have been taken from another song, as this surely can't be what they were playing or listening to at the time, but either way, an appealing frequency for all.

Tori Amos - Cornflake Girl   ‡

So, apparently, the piano is a boring instrument only fit for symphonic music or at the very most jazz? No way! In pop music, virtuosity is a rare and precious thing and this American artist reached its peak. She can instantly conjure up four motifs in a single song and the ease with which she handles Her instrument is charming. We just listen and admire!

Toad the Wet Sprocket - Fall Down   ~

With their name taken from a Monty Python sketch, you would expect this to be more quirky, but it is surprisingly safe for 'alternative'. The video seems much heavier than the actual song but the chorus and repeating riff gets trapped within you, so much, in fact, that the repeat button becomes your new best friend.

Prong - Whose Fist Is It Anyway?   *

I remember this like it was yesterday. A shoe box full of tapes and an offer: "My ex left it here, take whatever you want." I needed something to kick-start me and reset my head. One was marked 'Cleansing', which sounded like the right choice. After a few-weeks' long procedure rendered by Prong, I had an idea what might be happening in purgatory. I don't want to go there.

Satchel - Mr. Pink   +

I'm lying on my deathbed and a priest is coming to me. He puts a tablet in my hands and speaks with a decorous voice: "Choose a song you would like to hear for the last time. Regrettably, there is no more time left." I falter with quite a few. Then I see this one on the list. I press play. The song comes to an end. And I suddenly cannot wait for the heavens.

The Offspring - Self Esteem   +

Treating boys like puppets is what girls from the category of 'mega-bitches' do. In spite of all the effort from the guy, he always remains on the side track. Why does he always put up with that? The answer is provided by a punk song which probes the mind patterns of such a suffering lad. So, thank you for being bitches! Without you, this hit would not have been written.

Eric's Trip - Girlfriend   *

If punks can get lost in dreams, then dreamers are also able to rebel. It is clear to them that a good song is a good song even if it sounds like it was recorded in a bathroom on a tape recorder bought at a garage sale. They would shoot a video with their pocket money from grandma, but with grace; they might even have some shrapnel left for a beer. No wonder they made the people at Sub Pop fall to the floor in amazement.

Johnny Cash - Delia's Gone   ~

The greatest songs are simple; just a man and his guitar and a soul to to create beautiful words with and the ability to tell stories. Since the invention of the guitar, this formula has not been improved upon, and this fine example shows that this works in any era. Delia may have gone, but this song never will.

The Almighty - Jonestown Mind *

'Crank' is a whack with a guitar over your head. An album on which a bunch of pissed-off folk ignited their garage noise with no embellishment and, with no poetic metaphores, shouted out all that got on their tits. It won't do much for your intellectual enrichment but, when listening to it, you will get to meet your neighbours and squeeze 150 mph out of your rusty bone shaker on the highway.

Bailter Space - X +

The magical sound of a Rickenbacker guitar and a talent to create noisy layers of original melodies. The charm of this song's appeal comes from behind a waving curtain of alter-reality, as if the essence of beauty of human beings were sitting on the edge of peripheral vision, and you are trying to focus your gaze on it through the dirt of the world around. It is difficult, but worth it.

Beastie Boys - Sabotage ×

A proper bass, an energetic guitar, powerful drums, and angry screaming vocals – that calls for three hip-hoppers. A dynamic cut, an action motion picture camera, fake moustaches, and a couple of dummies – that calls for a good director. And the result? A legendary video. Five MTV VMA nominations. No award in the end? Sabotaaaage!

Method Man - Release Yo' Delf   *

The first rap album I ever listened to was 'Tical'. It is surrounded by a sinister aura of the 'hood after midnight; that is why pseudo gangstas dripping with gold and showing off their big cars in videos do not really win me over. A trumpeter is triumphantly announcing the coming of a new order. A resolute and respected ruler, who will enthrone it, has just arrived.

Dave Matthews Band - Satellite   ~

When you see or hear this band's name, you feel safe. Not known for going crazy with experimentation or pushing new boundaries, these are the types of bands you need in your life when you want that comfort blanket. And who would have thought this young brooding handsome teen would go on to be a hugely famous geek.

Samiam - Stepson   *

A compelling unity of sound and picture. Nothing missing, nothing redundant. An eagerly playing band with a story of a family drama compiled from stylised fragments of the plot. A simple play on light, colours, and shadows visually amplifies a fantastic emotionally gradually building song. No sentiment or mushiness, only a cathartic experience.

Failure - Undone   +

Was it just a precious experiment or an inspiration from above? Placing the bass guitar in the main role, enhancing its sound through boxes for sound distortion, and making the guitar a supporting character is a courageous decision. This resulted in music that does not compare. However, you can't go wrong if you try.

Oasis - Live Forever   ~

How can a band become so huge with such a big following, when they only seem to use three chords? Well, first take a man who has so much attitude that you are scared to even hold the CD. Then take his brother whose ear for music and writing skills are simply inspiring. This will now make their music live forever.

Ween - Voodoo Lady   *

Trying to guess how the next song on a Ween record will sound is like betting on a draw in basketball. When the lust for experimentation and a bizarre sense of humour were being handed out, they were first in line. Instead of sitting in a lesson on political correctness, they went for a fag. An explosion of creativity and a cabaret of crazy ideas, all in one.

The Black Crowes - Wiser Time ~

As a non-American, it's hard to have an "American dream" but I have always wanted to just get in a car and cruise across the whole of the country. This video encapsulates those desires and makes for one awesome driving song. It's about the adventure for me that the road will bring; people, places, and memories.

Meat Puppets - We Don't Exist *

If someone told me they played in a band which combines influences of punk, country, folk, and southern rock, I would just laugh him off. What would sound like an undigestable mess by others, the Kirkwood brothers nonchalantly deliver with a huge dose of charm. A big thanks to Kurt and Krist for helping me discover Curt and Cris.

Everything But the Girl
- Missing (Todd Terry Club Mix) +

When some people leave, total emptiness can be left in our lives. In the labyrinth of our own memories, we try to locate the places where we were still together. A strong message about clinging onto the past and the inability to move on in life. Fortunately, the sad lyrics are illuminated with a ray of hope through great music with a house beat.

The Cranberries - Zombie «

Thirty years of conflict in the British Isles ended just weeks after the release of this song, and it serves as a powerful reminder of a dark period in Anglo-Irish history. Condemning the mindset of young men fighting an endless battle using the weapons of fear and terror, its message remains extremely potent today.

Jawbox - Savory *

An attempt to move from the indie scene into the world of big business is not usually pleasant. Die-hard fans do not forgive such a betrayal and do not hide their disgust. 'Jawbox' withstood it with honour and recorded their best album – an electrifying duel of two raucous six strings roused with a driving rhythm section. It is not the logo on the cover that matters but the music that lays within the grooves.

Dog Eat Dog - No Fronts ~

With no serious message, no soft harmonies, no 'changed my life' moments, rock meets rap and rhyme with just a bunch of guys saying what they want. Addictive to the ears without being overkill and has surprising layers when listened to again. They cut out the fat and only leave the meat; just fun with no fronts.

Machine Head - Old *

Will love and truth win over hatred and lies? Can fire only be fought with fire and, if you turn the other cheek, will you get slapped? This band is clear on that. They get their own back on the world around them in their own way – with a breath taking insistence and zero compromises. A brutal reveille for those days when I get the feeling things can't get any worse. But they can!

Priessnitz - Hlavou dolů +

Local patriots from Jeseníky, who invocate the charm and the darkness of their native region with their music. Their mornings have no dawn. Amicable during the day but, at night, a frightening Gothic forest becomes their asylum, where they wander around impersonated into lumps of milky fog. In the end, they also creep into your temple, extinguish the flames of all the obsolete candles, and let their aura fully sparkle.

Bush - Comedown ~

This is a good song, but it becomes a great song when played acoustically. Bush was not a band I had listened to, until I heard them perform on a benefit CD. A more soulful, brilliantly constructed, well-written poesy you'll struggle to find. It is rare. I'd recommend a non-original, but check out the acoustic version!

Renegade Soundwave - Renegade Soundwave *

This sound wave always puts me in vacation mood, no matter the reality behind the window. I'm walking on the beach with a dewy glass in my hand, sand crunching between my toes, and I keep checking the swimming suits around me. The sun is tanning my teeth because I'm grinning from ear to ear and my troubles are burried at the bottom of the sea. It does not even have to be in Morocco.

Nine Inch Nails - March Of The Pigs ~

Possibly the strangest time signature ever. From the start it sounds out of time, but yet somehow it's in time the whole way through. Just when you start to understand, it's over, so you go for another listen, and realise that it's better than before. Some songs are meant to be heard, not understood, as this shows.

Lisa Germano - Cry Wolf *

The human mind is tricky. Desires and thoughts are tempting and can be a trap from which there is no escape. Because nothing comes for free and the price for a fulfilled wish can be scary. Who to blame then? If we are in charge of our own happiness, who owns the misfortune? A suggestive contrition where no one's guilty. But no one's innocent either.

Downset. - Anger +

The riot in LA left the deepest wounds in those who experienced it first hand. No pose, just a harsh ordeal for the rest of their life. A resonant, inconsolable anger rising from helplessness. How good then, that there is music as a way to express oneself. A mixture of hip hop, hardcore punk, and heavy metal. An adequate background for the described atrocity.

Soundgarden - Black Hole Sun ×

Only very few videos from the '90s can I remember better. Even now I can see every snapshot, every unusual picture, and also the uninvolved expressions of the band. It's the case when you listen to a song and see the video whether you like it or not. A precious, powerful interplay of music and picture. I still have no idea what the lyrics are about, but I don't mind.

Built to Spill - In the Morning *

The songs on this album don't make it clear what follows after their first verse and the chorus; in some cases it's not even clear what the verse is and what is the chorus. They are quirkily twisted, and the naughty ideas in them come and go as they please. The first reader for all who wish to know what 'indie rock' actually is.

Dodgy - Staying Out For The Summer ~

Undercooked sausages on a BBQ which you know you'll regret eating, the sea too cold to swim in but you still do, fighting off wasps for your beer, and sunburn so painful it hurts to look at. I love English summers, and this track takes me right back there. Simple, fun loving, and carefree – the summers and the song.

Arcwelder - Smile *

The best concerts I have ever been to were not seen by many. A small club, an unknown band, and a handful of fans, curious what will be shown. But some unique constellation occurred and the evening turned out to be smashing. The band played a dream set and I left happy. I haven't seen Arcwelder live, but I reckon it would be a superb gig.

Hole - Miss World +

"Cleanliness is next to godliness." The headline above the stage is an allusion to the use of barbiturates in the background of beauty contests. It is difficult to smile at the world and be beautiful when you feel empty inside. In such a moment, instead of a put-on smile, Courtney shows the middle finger. Although vulgar, for me the only 'Miss World' of the grunge scene.

Stiltskin - Inside　~

Some adverts make you want to buy a product, some entice you to visit somewhere, but I remember one for jeans that just made me want to buy the song. I wasn't the only person, it went to number one! The anthem for a generation of easily seduced teens that, today, wish they could still fit 'inside' those jeans.

Dinosaur Jr. - Feel the Pain　*

An unusual, as if almost 'indifferent' approach to singing, guitar riffs with an extra portion of fluffy feedback, and unmistakeable solos which may assault the ears, but I do not know any better. Maybe not their best album but, for me, forever the first one I heard. It starts with this brilliant song, which opened the gates to the introvert world of mister J. Mascis for me.

Korn - Shoots and Ladders　~

An innocent child singing their nursery rhymes without a care in the world. A father listening to his favourite band sing the same nursery rhymes, but without a trace of any innocence. All stories and rhymes have a meaning, and Korn tell these in their unique way, combining real metal with real passion and gusto.

Chumbawamba - Timebomb *

The punks of the dance floor, merry anarchists and provocateurs releasing their protest songs on a major label. Well, some people can't see the wood for the trees. Their guns were agitating leaflets rather than rifles and, while listening to them, you would rather have fun than organise riots. Jesters are allowed to say what others are too scared to think.

Bez ladu a skladu - Parné valce +

Cult representatives of the Slovak underground. Critics of the 'iron curtain' and the communistic system. Their music was the complete opposite of the grey regime. Provocative lyrics from the young front-man, the image of the band deviating from common outlines, and expressive cacophonic music made them into stars for a rebelling youth calling for change.

Green Day - Basket Case ×

Therapy for neurotics by Dr. Punk-rock, live from the asylum. I just love how the bass and drums nail it when they join the singer and his guitar in the first chorus, the bridge fits there like a butt on a bog. But I only fully enjoy it when it's together with the video. Such noise from psychiatric patients is not a common thing to see.

Girls Against Boys - Kill The Sexplayer *

If a bass makes the music, two basses can shake your guts. Especially if a precise drummer places every hit exactly where it belongs. The voice of Scott McCloud raises respect. He weights his words austerely, every single one declaimed with a chilly insistence. This is not an uncontrolled typhoon, but a thoroughly ingenious attack and aimed at your senses.

Blur - Parklife ~

When the lead singer doesn't feature heavily on one of their biggest songs, you may worry, but it was a masterstroke, as Damon didn't feel he would do it justice. The Cockney vocals elevate this to a song for the people; it becomes easy to sing along to, so much in fact, I won a karaoke competition with my rendition.

The Wedding Present - Yeah Yeah Yeah Yeah Yeah *

In my life I have accomplished many silly things, done a lot of wacky stuff, and conceived some sensational nonsense. All this, for one simple reason – I felt I just had to. What would you do if your head says a hundred times 'No!', but your heart says five times 'Yeah!'? The guy who wrote this knows how it feels when you lose your mind.

Public Enemy - Give It Up +

The clowns of a cruel truth; two of them serious, and one at quarter to seven – original artists with a great logo. They mock gangsters' lies, they do not care about poses, expensive alcohol or cigars. Give up the illusion of heroes who wear bulletproof vests even in the shower. Save the youth, read books, and listen to Public Enemy!

Shed Seven - Ocean Pie ~

Complex guitars, wailing vocals, and technical brilliance saw these as one of the forefathers of Britpop. Future bands were bigger by being simpler but these remain best to me. No CD collection is complete without this album in which every song delivers. At first listen, you like it, second listen: love it forever.

Come - In/Out *

Sometimes you go out with friends just to have fun. Other times you know in advance that, instead of fun, your evening will be about empathy, understanding, and providing support to an unhappy close person. With Come, you should prepare likewise. Behind the wall of screeching guitars lie the worries of one soul tested by life, worth listening to.

The Cult - Coming Down (Drug Tongue) ~

A full in the face musical experience, which has an explosive video to match. The thumping bassline backbone, the highly charged and distorted guitars, and the pumping ferocious drums leave no room for any delicateness or finesse. But none is needed; the rawness pushes through and leaves you wanting more.

Pavement - Cut Your Hair *

They play as if they have just learned how to and are trying to find out what to do with it. Although, they really can play. They sing as if they do not care much. But they are smarter than they look. They sound quite sloppy, even though they know exactly what they are doing. Do not let them go in one ear and out the other. Otherwise, you will not discover that they are more entertaining than you first thought.

Senser - The Key +

A fusion of distorted metal guitar parts, the bass walking along in the background accompanying the hippie drums. Add scratches from an old turntable and intelligent lyrics of the frontman which are full of metaphors enriched with a female vocal from 'One Thousand and One Nights'. Everything fits together like a lock mechanism. The key to opening it, you have in your hands.

Mighty Mighty Bosstones - Hell of a Hat *

The '90s favoured attempts to combine various music genres. A successful breed of hopping ska and vigorous punk let a whole new scene be born. Boston's pioneers of ska-punk added an extra brass section and occasional metal raids. They have enough sound variety to avoid monotony and are mighty, mighty entertaining.

Melvins - Revolve ~

In homage to the Blues Brother's; a net to protect the band from glasses being thrown, although the singer's hair would probably have been big enough. The singer carries his head around like a handbag, there is a bizarre tap dancing cowboy and the crowd would be better at a boxing match. Truly crazy, but truly great.

Kristin Hersh - Your Ghost *

Fragile tones of acoustic guitar are pervaded with ceremonial silence, a voice full of emotion caresses the heart, yet, it sends shivers down the spine. Our loved ones remain with us forever. They may have left, but they haven't closed the door and, through its crack, they keep coming to visit in our thoughts. The trails of memories of them are indelibly imprinted on the doormat.

Slobodná Európa - Podvod   +

What doesn't kill you makes you stronger. With this punk rock band it is perhaps twice as true. It is a small wonder that this great song, and actually the whole second album, was created at all. The band got empowered by the drug demon back then. Dark music and bleak lyrics are portraying a perfect picture of that time. But the lyrics of the song 'Podvod' are current to this day.

Corrosion of Conformity - Albatross   *

Formerly fierce hardcore punks who larded their socially critical testimonies with thrash metal, detouring through heavy metal off-shoot towards groovy stoner rock? I'm not a big fan of genre tumbles but when a double somersault with a clean landing on the feet is delivered, I have to applaud. It is as if they never played anything else.

Weezer - Buddy Holly   ~

You will not find any depth in the lyrics, there is no stunning guitar solo and if you want some amazing percussion, look elsewhere. Stay here only to watch one of the greatest music videos ever, which mixes a classic TV show with a, now, classic tune. Sometimes, just being funny is better than just being good.

Killing Joke - Pandemonium   *

Yet again there came a time when the world's end is, supposedly, only a few weeks away. Jaz Coleman has been warning before the approaching apocalypse for ages. He would not find a better band to musicalise his visions and the performance of secret ceremonies and ritual dances. With a muscular rhythm section, pounding riffs, and oriental motifs, it would be a stylish end.

Ash - Uncle Pat   +

I am an uncle. I have a cottage in the middle of a picturesque wood. But my nephew, unfortunately, does not have a rock band, so he hasn't written a tune about the beauty of that place; not yet, anyway. Though he could shower me with handfuls of nostalgic memories already. Still, I get to listen to this lyrical song by Ash and imagine it is about me and written for me.

Underworld - Dirty Epic   *

Another argument that shattered my prejudices. And my belief that nothing apart from guitar music is worth it and electronica is the music to ban. The images may give you a seizure but try closing your eyes and surrendering to the hypnotic sound. The world will become a carefree place where the only thing that matters is dancing.

Pulp - Lipgloss ~

Jarvis Cocker's incomparable vocals stood out when these '90s Britpop bands ran wild. His crazy hand gestures only serve to entice you into the song more, but don't try it yourself, you will look foolish. I can still smell those smoky and sweaty nightclubs now where we gathered to show this music is hard to dance to.

The Jon Spencer Blues Explosion - Bellbottoms *

They are wild, conceited, and they are most assured of the fact that no one around can play better rock'n'roll. Hence, they can afford to play an ode to bell-bottoms without sounding embarrassing while doing so. Conversely, with their dedication and attitude, they are able to convince that it is a must to have at least one pair at home. Cocksure guys like these just have to know that.

Sugartooth - Sold My Fortune +

A young band riding the wave of grunge. A well-singing frontman fairly good at playing the guitar. The lead guitarist plays charmingly inventive riffs. The drummer has a huge talent and hits the kit hard. This video was aired in the cult MTV series Beavis & Butthead. What was missing that they did not make it big? An explanation comes with the song title.

Nas - Halftime *

What more can be written about a song from the soundtrack to the movie 'Zebrahead', about which a twenty-page essay has already been published? The ferocious youngster, back then still Nasty Nas, used it to knock on the gates of the rap Olympus in 1992. At the time, they only curiously peeked through the peephole but, two years later, when he released 'Illmatic', they opened the door wide.

Live - I Alone ~

They are still being discovered by many today and liked as much now as back then. It's as near to perfection as possible with no complications or hidden agendas, just a simple message: To discover the truth, or at least a truth you want to believe, then don't listen to words of others. I found it for myself, I alone.

Medicine - Time Baby III *

I borrowed the soundtrack to 'The Crow' on an old cassette tape. It was so worn that I didn't even dare to make a copy and it was so great I didn't want to return it either. In the crowd of big names and stellar songs, Medicine, who I had never heard of before, furtively stole the show with this gorgeous tune.

Mark Lanegan - House a Home ~

The greats are great for being themselves; Mark was in many good bands and accompanied some of the best, but his solo stuff showed why he didn't 'need' to have others. You can get lost but still find yourself in his music as he expresses the pain he has lived through, more than a lifetime's worth for most.

Kyuss - Demon Cleaner *

When four out of your four flatmates listen to sterile pop and disco techno, your psychological health is threatened. Therefore, the ritual cleansing moments for me were when I would move the armchair in front of our giant speakers in the blacked-out living room and let myself be pushed into it by the hurricane of massive Kyuss sound. Musical exorcism in practice.

Lagwagon - Island of Shame *

"You should start at full speed and then just accelerate", our gym teacher used to say. I guess he also taught these guys. Just play the first song and you know immediately what to expect from the rest of the playing time. Unrestrained blasts in breakneck tempos, several stoptimes per track, and vocals that are a pleasure to scream out of the window of a speeding car.

The Coup - Fat Cats, Bigga Fish *

Where some fight for their belief with uproar and rage, The Coup choose to use their arsenal of flowing funky beats and sarcastic word play. They are openly political and do not hide their leftist ideas between the lines. Like in this story of a small-time burglar, who discovers that major league theft is played out somewhere else.

Liz Phair - Supernova *

Discussed, praised, execrated, loved, and also hated. A calculating bitch who only aimed for loads of money from the beginning, or just a talented author who tried to take an opportunity? In any case, poignant, provocative, playful, and sexy, capable of writing an interesting song. And in '94, also still indie and wearing no bra.

King's X - Dogman *

One of those bands whose name excites appreciating head nodding of many; however, only a few have actually heard their album. So I gave it a try myself. 'Dogman' stunned me with terrific riffs, soul soaked vocals, a rock solid rhythm section, and a really heavy sound. If you wish to verify the praising rumours one day around King's X, start right here.

Complete playlists

The following playlists include songs whose videos were covered in the individual chapters – not just those to which QR codes can be found above, but also all those to which videos are currently available on the official profiles of the artists and their publishers. We hope you enjoy this ride, several hours long, full of musical discovery.

1990

1991

1992

1993

1994

Conclusion

Like most revolutions, the musical one that came about in the first half of the '90s also had a violent course and a short duration. For a moment, however, it stirred up the waters of the mainstream and brought in not only a little excitement and noise but especially artistic authenticity. It did not break out for no reason; it was necessitated by the stagnation of sales of albums and the consequent effort of publishers to find new ways of attracting the listeners to buy them. Thus, they turned their attention to the diverse world of music subcultures which, until then, only occurred on the fringes of commercial interest.

There, they discovered unexpected potential and brought to the surface such artists and bands who managed to reach a new generation of listeners. They no longer enjoyed listening to the slick production of mainstream radio, as it was too far removed from the reality they lived on a daily basis, and it did not refer to the issues they were faced with in their own lives. That is why they were looking for an alternative in the form of music that would speak directly to them and that they would be able to identify with.

Music videos proved to be an effective tool for communicating with this young audience and, along with them, the format of music TV programmes and stations gained importance. Among them, MTV built a literally opinion-forming position. Any video broadcast and subsequently included in the daily rotation had an immediate impact on the sales of recordings. MTV, thus, became a key medium for the spread of new sound trends. If it had not been for its influence, it would be hard to imagine an explosion of popularity of alternative rock, hip-hop, or grunge to the extent it occurred in the early '90s.

In this period, major record companies expanded their catalogues to include minority genres, either by signing directly with artists or through distribution agreements with independent labels. They spent quite a lot of resources on their promotion and, thus, a wide spectrum of diverse music reached the common listener. Thanks to this, there was an opportunity to get to know such music as a malleable form of artistic expression that does not have to be just an easily digestible product or a means of cheap entertainment.

In terms of content, music turned out to be a vital tool for social commentary and deep personal statements. Hip-hop bands used it to open up burning topics, troubling not only the population living on the outskirts and in the ghettos of big cities. They pointed to social inequality, racism, street violence, and drug crime, often all in a highly concentrated form within a single song. Alternative rock bands, on the other hand, emotionally developed the themes of searching for one's own identity, a place in society, and the resulting feelings of uncertainty or frustration.

Serious motives of dissatisfaction, pain, or disappointment in the work of alternative artists of the first half of the '90s were balanced out by their musical diversity. The era was favourable for bringing together such subcultures that, until that point, were rather diverse. This was helped not only by the emergence of multi-genre music festivals but also by MTV's varied programming, uniting music fans of all kinds. The interlinking and intermingling of rock, hip-hop, punk, pop, metal, and electronica also bore quality fruit, although some newly formed offshoots did not last long, and others were only transitional stages to other, more viable varieties.

Of the many genres determining the music direction of this period, the first half of the '90s culminated in particularly strong stories of hip-hop and grunge. Their example shows that remarkable music forms mostly lie beneath the surface of mass interest. However, until the seeds of raw thoughts and sound ideas developed, after years of trial and error, into novelties with the potential to appeal to broad masses of listeners, it required not only time but also favourable conditions. These were concentrated around concert clubs and especially independent record labels.

This infrastructure, essential for the formation of local communities and the establishment of music bands, would not have worked without countless hours of enthusiastic self-help activities in the background. Promoters and publishers often came from the ranks of fans or played in bands themselves, attended concerts of their fellow musicians, and, in this way, helped strengthen the cohesion of the scene. Although both hip-hop and grunge originated from such an environment, the course, and especially the impact of their journeys from the underground to the limelight, differed.

Hip-hop slowly made its way into the wider consciousness and built a following from the early '80s. It developed simultaneously in several places, with epicentres in New York City on the east and the Los Angeles area on the west coast of the USA. Despite regional specificities, these two areas shared a common cultural and musical foundations and the fierce rivalry between them helped the whole scene to grow. The genre gradually planted its roots outside of traditional strongholds and, between the end of the '80s and the first half of the '90s, it experienced a period of commercial and artistic prosperity that went down in music history as the 'golden age of hip-hop'.

Grunge, on the other hand, became a sensation literally overnight. This was helped by the clever marketing policy of its home label Sub Pop and a once-in-a-century record. This small scene, territorially situated in a single place, was not prepared for such a situation. The sudden success, as well as the attention of fans and media from around the world, put enormous pressure on the handful of bands at its forefront. They did not find it easy to cope with such enormous popularity and, for one of them, the collision with fame had fatal consequences.

Kurt Cobain's tragic death in the spring of 1994 was like a cold shower not only for the numerous fans but also for the scene itself. *Nirvana* definitively ended their career after this event, *Pearl Jam* decided to withdraw into seclusion. *Alice in Chains* cancelled a planned tour just a day before it was to start due to their singer's worsening drug addiction, only to stop touring altogether. *Mudhoney* had always been too weird for the mainstream, *TAD* was too uncouth; thus, the crown of the kings of Seattle was taken over by *Soundgarden*, who continued to tour in the coming months. Nevertheless, grunge as a cohesive scene ceased to exist.

Hip-hop, on the other hand, had brighter prospects ahead. Subsequent albums by *Wu-Tang Clan*, *A Tribe Called Quest*, and *Cypress Hill* all went platinum, while *2Pac* and *Nas* debuted at the top of the album chart with their new records. The hip-hop scene was not spared several tragic deaths of leading figures either but, unlike grunge, it did not have a liquidating effect on it, rather the opposite. Although it did not avoid periods of stagnation in later years, it has maintained its position as a current and relevant music entity to this day.

Even though the worlds of the value-oriented underground and the entertainment industry have been incompatible for a long time, in the first half of the '90s, their paths briefly crossed. The steep penetration of music originating from the independent scene to the waves of the mainstream was soon to be accompanied by a fundamental discrepancy between artistic ideals and the rules of the functioning of show business.

During this period of 'the search for a new Nirvana', major labels offered indie bands lucrative contracts with the promise of respecting their artistic freedom. When signing them, they often did not realise the generous budgets for recording, promotion, or concert tours were just an advance from the expected future profits of their recordings. If they did not sell enough, the bands got in debt with the labels and, as a result, became prisoners of their own contracts. Such labels, expecting a return on their investment, measured the quality of recordings by strict commercial criteria. Had these not been fulfilled, they cut down on not only marketing support but also on their willingness not to interfere in the artistic process. Hence, it was primarily the artists who got the short end of the stick.

The artists coped with the reality of planned returns and commercial pressure in different ways. Some chose a compromise of 'softening' the edges of their work in an attempt to meet the expectations of their audiences, even at the cost of losing individuality, others tried to get out of contractual obligations through legal means. However, the adventure with the music business led many to end their activities or, at best, to return to where they came from – the underground. In turn, many excellent titles fell into oblivion in the catalogues of major labels, as they, due to unprofitability, did not receive the care they deserved.

Artists moving from independent to major labels also fuelled debate about the sustainability of artistic credibility and authenticity in a commercial environment. After signing a contract, most of them faced strong resentment, or even a boycott, from their own core fans, as well as accusations of selling out. Even though marketing support and the possibility of performing concerts on larger stages alongside well-known names allowed them to introduce themselves to a wider audience, they lost contact with the environment that had shaped them and it, in many cases, was an important basis and inspiration for their work.

This manifested in the raw sound of their recordings, the sincerity of their lyrical statements and was also transferred to the specific aesthetics of the video clips. The music captured undisguised emotions, undiluted passion, sadness, and anger, real blood, sweat and tears, as it was not concerned with whether someone would like it or not. It is, thus, hard to imagine that, in conditions where the amount of the reward, or the debt incurred, depends on the number of albums sold, it would be possible to save face in the long term and not slip into the trap of gambling on the music tastes of the audience.

Therefore, for orthodox fans, a contract with a major publishing house was tantamount to artistic suicide. The way in which Kurt Cobain ended his life can be seen as a literal fulfilment of this metaphor. The extremity and definitive irreversibility of his act momentarily shook not only fans but also the entire music world and forced everyone to consider why it had to happen. Symbolically, he proved the sceptics who claimed that a career in the entertainment industry would not bring much happiness to artists with an independent spirit were right.

● ● ●

After the tumultuous events at the beginning of the '90s, its second half felt and sounded different. Alternative artists had breathed fresh air into the stagnant music industry, reignited record sales and set new sound trends in the mainstream. Their followers were already coming to an environment where there was a strong demand for alternative music.

All that was necessary to satisfy a mainstream listener who wanted to hear more new music with a particular sound was recycle successful practices. The sound concept of grunge and alternative rock was taken over by post-grunge, nu-metal developed from metal influences, hip-hop felt really at home in the commercial sphere. An incredible increase in the music on offer passed off as alternative caused this label to lose its original meaning, which naturally required other alternatives. The genre spectrum of the mainstream was brightened by the positive charge of pop punk, lightened by the irony and insight of Britpop, while electronica claimed the floor in a louder and louder way. The third wave of ska was rolling through the independent scene, swing was experiencing its revival, hardcore was regaining its former respect, emo was beckoning with its heart on its sleeve, and post rock was pushing the horizons of instrumental music.

The rise of the internet fundamentally changed the ways music was spread and promoted, cassette tapes and vinyl definitively gave up under the supremacy of CDs. As the digital mp3 format became more and more popular, the sharing of digital music files came into play. MTV went through dramatic changes and gradually lost its supremacy as an opinion-forming medium, the music industry had to find new ways to deal with technological advances and a new generation of music listeners. But let us save all that for another time.

Offenses against methodology

Even though, in the introduction of this book, we stated a rather rigid methodology, it would only be honest to admit we did not manage to adhere to all the points one hundred percent. In at least three cases, we violated one of our own terms and conditions.

The book only includes such songs for which an official video was filmed and broadcast or otherwise published. There are, however, two exceptions. The first one was partially broken by *Pearl Jam* and was included with our full awareness. When their third studio album, *Vitalogy*, was released in 1994, they were rather reticent in their communication with the media; they neither gave interviews, nor shot any videos. They were still one of the most in-demand concert bands in the world, but their activity was marred by a gruelling lawsuit against a company called Ticketmaster. In it, they pointed out unfair practices in the pricing of concert tickets, as well as monopolistic behaviour in the long-term contracting of concert venues.

The absence of videos from this period was partially amended by the director Cameron Crowe on the occasion of the band's twentieth anniversary. In his documentary *Pearl Jam Twenty* (2011), he also included a music video for the song *Not For You*, which he edited from contemporary concert and archive footage. He captured the band playing at their peak, in a raw live version of one of their most powerful songs. Therefore, although the video was created 17 years after the album's release, it clearly belongs in this book.

The second case occurred due to negligence. In addition to the excellent soundtrack, several music videos were released to promote the film *The Crow* (1994). Thus, there was no reason to suspect that the one by *Medicine* was not official, especially since the band itself appears in it for a moment. However, it was just a clever montage of scenes from the film in the form of a trailer. The footage of *Medicine* came directly from the film, where they played a concert band and performed *Time Baby*. However, not the 'number III' version, which is on the soundtrack and the track is also used in the video in question, but its predecessor, 'number II', released a year earlier on the *5ive* mini-album.

Since this is a great song and *Medicine* did not release any other record in 1994 for which they would shoot a video, we kept it in the selection. Hence, the video for *Time Baby III* appears here as a tribute to fan creativity and, at the same time, the only unofficial exception, confirming the methodological rule.

In the introductory text of each chapter, we only refer to bands and artists who, during their active career, recorded at least one video. Except for one. When it comes to the alternative music scene, there are few artists who are spoken of with as much reverence and respect as *Fugazi*. This band stubbornly adhered to the principles of independence throughout their musical career and, despite many offers from major record companies, they remained true to their philosophy.

They released their records on their own label and earned a living by selling records and playing concerts. They refused to sell non-musical products bearing their name, as well as to give interviews to major media outlets. Therefore, just as their fans could not buy official T-shirts with their logo, they would also wait in vain for their video on MTV. The band did not approve of either of these forms of promotion and refused to participate in them; thus, no *Fugazi* music video can be found. However, their great admirer Eddie Vedder used a small trick to sneak their name onto the TV screen; so a mention of them quite deservedly appeared in this book as well.

About the authors

Rasťo
I have always liked to discover new, unnoticed, or forgotten music and enthusiastically shared it with anyone who was willing to listen to me talking about it passionately, without any genre prejudices. By means of this book, I wanted to pay homage to music, as well as try to give it back some of the positive energy it gave me throughout my life.

Shezz
Brought up on '70s and '80s rock, which I still love, it was in the '90s when I found my feet as well as grunge. So, if grunge is now dead, when should I hang up my plaid shirts and cut my hair? Well, not just yet, for as long as this book exists, so do my fond memories and the potential to be what and whoever I wish.

Zebra
Music is my drug, my passion, and my love. It is a way of intimate communication. It allows me to travel in time and space and to get to know myself through emotions. It fills me when I'm empty and frees me when I'm fed up. In real life, I'm a big horse dressed in striped pyjamas who, in addition to music, likes tried and tested foods and wines.

Aran
Above all, I would like to say this book would not have been created without Rasťo and his enthusiasm and passion. Those are exactly the attributes I understand when it comes to music – enthusiasm and passion. I am similarly 'unhinged'. I grew up on punk and Pink Floyd and I wouldn't change that. Yes, the '90s were great but what's going on now is much, much better.

Veni

I grew up listening to punk and metal and, later, also to pop, synthpop, and electronica. I like music, I live it, and I feel it more than I can write about it. Still, many great songs go unnoticed in the flood of the production preferred by labels and radio stations. Therefore, my mission is to bring people to listen to them.

Kubsson

He already has the new album! Retractable pencil saves the batteries in the Walkman. No children's choirs in choruses! A VHS filled with music videos. He can't be dead, there's no way. Yes, I want a pack of blank CDs for Christmas. Why have I ignored this band until now? Mp3 or FLAC? The cover version is better than the original. Auto-reverse is great.

Iva

Music has been in my life since my early childhood. First as a subject of my curiosity when I felt the need to try to play different musical instruments. Later on, through fascination with its universality – a language that knows no borders and needs no words. Still, everything can be said with it. Just listen really closely.

Julian

Most people look back at their formative years as the peak of their musical appreciation, however, I feel like I'm living it now. Undeterred by previous influences of social cliques and fashion choices depending on who you listened to, I now have carte blanche to sit back and just enjoy the music.

Acknowledgements

This book was not planned. It came into the world by itself, as a result of the natural development of events and the interplay of favourable circumstances. Its final form was, directly or indirectly, influenced by a number of important people who entered my life over the years. Each of them left their signature on one of the pages and they all deserve sincere thanks for that.

First of all, I would like to thank the entire team of authors – Mark Sherrington, Braňo Špirk, Adam Nenadál, Robo Vehner, Kubo Magál, Ivana Klučková, and Julian Duckworth. Without their energy, efforts, and especially their willingness to share their music-related memories and observations, this book would be much less interesting to read. Miro Preclík, a non-writing member of the group, has been taking care of Alternator's technical support for a long time and whenever there is anything that needs fixing, he is the one to do that.

When finalising the book, I had the opportunity to look, with admiration, into the world of language proofreading and graphic design. Ivana Vereski and Matúš Gamrat made sure the ideas of the English-speaking co-authors sounded as good in Slovak as they did in their native language. Zita Mihálıková kept an eye on correct grammar and style but was, at the same time, sensitive to our idiosyncrasies; making sure it sounded as we heard it in our heads. Milan Pleva breathed life into the book and made it not only pleasant to read but also easy to look at.

The original idea – to write this book in English – had to wait a few years for its realisation. Eva Eddy skilfully translated the ideas and words in the book while her husband Jonathan Eddy proofread the text and, also, noticed several factual inaccuracies, which the readers of the English version now do not have to scratch their heads over.

The opening chapter mentions characters whose resemblance to real people is not purely coincidental – Mr Peter Lurík from Roxy

Music Shop, the independent music distributor Klaus, and Jesus, a promoter of HC concerts. They influenced me forever with their warmth, friendliness, and contagious enthusiasm for music. The same qualities also go for Pišta Vandal, who was behind the decision to self-publish the book.

From a musical point of view, this book would not be half as good if it was not for several important sources of inspiration. Among them, there was the legendary Radio Ragtime, especially its presenters Daniel Baláž and Bohuš Kraus. It was in their programmes that I discovered many of the artists presented above. Apart from numerous music-related tips I got from the independent label Silver Rocket, I also learnt that, in addition to enthusiasm, the key to a good DIY approach is honest and persistent work. It helped me a lot in times when my writing went a bit off the rails.

Behind the varied mix of genres captured on the pages of this book there are many people who I allowed to draw me into the world of their favourite music over the years. Therefore, Juro, Remo, Jano, Milan, Važo, uncle Peter, the whole boy-scout gang, with whom I experienced my first pogoes, as well as all those who have enthusiastically passed an album onto me, or took me to a concert, should also be mentioned here.

Last but not least, my thanks go to my parents for the fact that a gramophone and records were a favourite cultural pastime in our house, which has remained with me to this day. Also, for the years of patience with the music, often surely not the most pleasant or comprehensible for them, that was always playing in my room. I owe my older brother for his musical curiosity and diverse taste, as a result of which, I grew up surrounded by all kinds of music without genre prejudices.

Special thanks go to Ivka for her trust and support in those times when I stopped believing in myself. Also, for her curious questions, thinking about which guided me in the right direction many a time. One of them also contributed to the concept of this book. Many thanks!

Translator's notes

*40 / Ride - Vapour Trail
Having asked what he meant here, Shezz said he wanted to leave the reader guessing/decide for themselves whether Ride were not good enough to match the big Britpop bands or they simply chose not to compete with them.

*43 / The La's - There She Goes
So, apparently, Shezz is referring to the film 'So I married an axe murderer' - who would've guessed, right?

*45 / Ice Cube - Who's the Mack
Even though hip-hop came out of inner-city areas, by the time Ice Cube was releasing records, it had moved to housing 'projects' that were located on the outskirts of big cities or urban areas and were almost exclusively inhabited by African Americans and other ethnic minorities.

*65 / Temple of the Dog - Hunger Strike
When this contribution was written, Chris Cornell was still alive.

*69 / Cypress Hill - Phuncky Feel One
Since the authors of the book were barely out of nappies themselves when they wrote this, they were not aware hip-hop had a much longer history and tradition than the records they were listening to.

*162 / Slowdive - Alison
"I can take despair. It's the hope I can't stand." is a quote taken from the film Clockwise (1986) directed by Christopher Morahan.

Index of included albums

2Pac - 2Pacalypse Now (Interscope Records, 1991) - *If My Homie Calls*

4 Non Blondes - Bigger, Better, Faster, More! (Interscope Records, 1992) - *What's Up*

Afghan Whigs, The - Gentlemen (Elektra, 1993) - *Gentlemen*

Alice In Chains - Facelift (Columbia, 1990) - *We Die Young*

Alice In Chains - Dirt (Columbia, 1992) - *Down in the Hole / Would?*

Alice In Chains - Jar of Flies EP (Columbia, 1994) - *No Excuses*

Almighty, The - Crank (Chrysalis, 1994) - *Jonestown Mind*

American Music Club - Everclear (Alias Records, 1991) – *Rise*

Amos, Tori - Little Earthquakes (Atlantic, 1992) - *Winter*

Amos, Tori - Under the Pink (Atlantic, 1994) - *Cornflake Girl*

Anthrax (feat. Public Enemy) - Attack of the Killer B's (Island Records, 1991) - *Bring the Noise*

Aphex Twin - On EP (Warp Records, 1993) - *On*

Arcwelder - Xerxes (Touch and Go, 1994) - *Smile*

Archers of Loaf - Icky Mettle (Alias Records, 1993) - *Might*

Ash - Trailer EP (Infectious Records, 1994) - *Uncle Pat*

Autechre - Basscadet EP (Warp Records, 1994) - *Basscadet*

Babes in Toyland - Fontanelle (Reprise Records, 1992) - *Bruise Violet*

Bad Religion - Generator (Epitaph, 1992) - *Atomic Garden*

Bad Religion - Recipe for Hate (Epitaph, 1993)

Bailter Space - Vortura (Matador, 1994) - *X*

Band of Susans - Veil (Restless Records, 1993) - *Blind*

Barkmarket - Gimmick (American Recordings, 1993) - *Whipping Boy*

Basehead - Play With Toys (Imago, 1992) - *Not Over You*

Bats, The - Fear of God (Flying Nun Records, 1991) - *The Black and Blue*

Beastie Boys - Check Your Head (Capitol Records, 1992) - *Jimmy James*

Beastie Boys - Ill Communication (Grand Royal, 1994) - *Sabotage*

Beat Happening - Dreamy (Sub Pop, 1991) - *Hot Chocolate Boy*

Beck - Mellow Gold (Geffen Records, 1994) - *Loser*

Belly - Star (4AD, 1993) - *Gepetto*

Bettie Serveert - Palomine (Guernica, 1992) - *Kid's Allright*

Bez ladu a skladu - Iba raz (BMG Ariola, 1994) - *Parné valce*

Biohazard - Urban Discipline (Roadrunner Records, 1992) - *Punishment*

Björk - Debut (One Little Indian, 1993) - *Venus as a Boy / Big Time Sensuality*

Black Crowes, The - Amorica (American Recordings, 1994) - *Wiser Time*

Blind Melon - Blind Melon (Capitol Records, 1992) - *Change / No Rain*

Blur - Leisure (Food Records, 1991) - *She's So High*

Blur - Modern Life Is Rubbish (Food Records, 1993) - *For Tomorrow*

Blur - Parklife (Food Records, 1994) - *Parklife*

Body Count - Body Count (Sire, 1992) - *There Goes the Neighborhood*

Body Count - Born Dead (Virgin Records, 1994) - *Necessary Evil*

Boo Radleys, The - Giant Steps – (Creation Records, 1993) - *Lazarus*

Brad - Shame (Epic, 1993) - *20th Century*

Breeders, The - Safari EP (4AD, 1992) - *Safari*

Breeders, The - Last Splash (4AD, 1993) – *Cannonball*

Buckley, Jeff - Grace (Columbia, 1994) - *Grace*

Buffalo Tom - Let Me Come Over (Situation Two, 1992) - *Taillights Fade*

Built to Spill - There's Nothing Wrong With Love (Up Records, 1994) - *In the Morning*

Bush - Sixteen Stone (Trauma Records, 1994) - *Machinehead / Comedown*

Butthole Surfers - Independent Worm Saloon (Capitol Records, 1993) - *Who Was in My Room Last Night*

Candlebox - Candlebox (Maverick, 1993) - *Cover Me*

Carter USM - 30 Something (Rough Trade, 1991) - *Bloodsport for All*

Carter USM - 1992: The Love Album (Chrysalis, 1992) - *Only Living Boy in New Cross*

Cash, Johnny - American Recordings (American Recordings, 1994) - *Delia's Gone*

Catherine Wheel - Ferment (Fontana, 1992) - *Black Metallic*

Clerks: Music from the Motion Picture (Columbia, 1994)

Cocteau Twins - Heaven or Las Vegas (4AD, 1990) - *Iceblink Luck*

Codeine - Barely Real (Sub Pop, 1992) – *Realize*

Cohen, Leonard - The Future (Columbia, 1992) - *The Future*

Collins, Edwyn - Gorgeous George (Setanta Records, 1994) - *A Girl Like You*

Come - Don't Ask, Don't Tell (Matador, 1994) - *In/Out*

Coneheads: Music From The Motion Picture Soundtrack (Warner Bros. Records, 1993) – Red Hot Chili Peppers - *Soul to Squeeze*

Corrosion of Conformity - Deliverance (Columbia, 1994) - *Albatross*

Cosmic Psychos - Palomino Pizza (Amphetamine Reptile, 1993) - *Rain Gauge*

Coup, The - Genocide & Juice - (Wild Pitch Records, 1994) - *Fat Cats, Bigga Fish*

Cows, The - Cunning Stunts (Amphetamine Reptile, 1992) - *Mine*

Cranberries, The - Everybody Else Is Doing It, So Why Can't We? (Island Records, 1993) - *Linger*

Cranberries, The - No Need to Argue (Island Records, 1994) - *Ridiculous Thoughts / Zombie*

Crow, The: Original Motion Picture Soundtrack (Atlantic, 1994) - Medicine - *Time Baby III*

Cult, The - The Cult (Beggars Banquet, 1994) - *Coming Down*

Cure, The - Wish (Fiction Records, 1992) - *High / Friday I'm in Love*

Curve - Doppelgänger (Anxious Records, 1992)

Curve - Cuckoo (Anxious Records, 1993) - *Superblaster*

Cypress Hill - Cypress Hill (Ruffhouse Records, 1991) - *The Phuncky Feel One*

Cypress Hill - Black Sunday (Ruffhouse Records, 1993) - *Insane in the Brain*

Dave Matthews Band - Under the Table and Dreaming (RCA, 1994) - *Satellite*

Davová psychóza - Antropofóbia (Opus, 1991) - *Mozgová paralýza*

Dead Can Dance - Into the Labyrinth (4AD, 1993) - *The Carnival Is Over*

Deee-Lite - World Clique (Elektra, 1990) - *Groove Is in the Heart*

Depeche Mode - Violator (Mute, 1990) - *Personal Jesus*

Depeche Mode - Songs of Faith and Devotion (Mute, 1993) - *I Feel You*

dEUS - Worst Case Scenario (Island Records, 1994) - *Suds & Soda*

DiFranco, Ani - Imperfectly (Righteous Babe Records, 1992) - *In or Out*

Dig - Dig (Radioactive, 1993) - *Believe*

Dinosaur Jr. - Green Mind (Warner Bros. Records, 1991) - *The Wagon*

Dinosaur Jr. - Without a Sound (Blanco y Negro, 1994) - *Feel the Pain*

Disposable Heroes of Hiphoprisy, The - Hypocrisy Is the Greatest Luxury (4th & Broadway, 1992) - *Television the Drug of a Nation*

Dodgy - Homegrown (A&M Records, 1994) - *Staying Out for the Summer*

Dog Eat Dog - All Boro Kings (Roadrunner Records, 1994) - *No Fronts*

Downset. - Downset (Mercury, 1994) - *Anger*

Dr. Dre - Chronic (Interscope Records, 1992) - *Let Me Ride*

Dunaj - Dudlay (Bonton, 1993) - *Jednou*

EMF - Schubert Dip (Parlophone, 1991) - *I Believe / Unbelievable*

Eric's Trip - Forever Again (Sub Pop, 1994) - *Girlfriend*

Everything But the Girl - Amplified Heart (Blanco y Negro, 1994) - *Missing (Todd Terry remix)*

Failure - Magnified (Slash Records, 1994) - *Undone*

Faith No More - Angel Dust (Slash Records, 1992) - *Everything's Ruined / Small Victory*

Fields of Nephilim - Elizium (Beggars Banquet, 1990) - *For Her Light*

Fishbone - The Reality of My Surroundings (Columbia, 1991) - *Sunless Saturday*

Flaming Lips, The - Transmissions from the Satellite Heart (Warner Bros. Records, 1993) - *Turn It On*

Fluid, The - Glue (Sub Pop, 1990) - *Black Glove*

For Love Not Lisa - Merge (EastWest Records, 1993) - *Slip Slide Melting*

Frank Black - Teenager of the Year (4AD, 1994) - *Headache*

Frente! - Marvin the Album (Mammoth Records, 1992) - *Ordinary Angels*

Front Line Assembly - Tactical Neural Implant (Third Mind Records, 1992) – *Mindphaser*

Future Sound of London, The - Lifeforms (Virgin, 1994)

Galactic Cowboys - Galactic Cowboys (Geffen Records, 1991) - *I'm Not Amused*

Gang Starr - Hard to Earn (Chrysalis, 1994)

Germano, Lisa - Geek the Girl (4AD, 1994) - *Cry Wolf*

Girl Trouble - New American Shame (Empty Records, 1993) - *My Hometown*

Girls Against Boys - Cruise Yourself (Touch and Go, 1994) - *Kill the Sexplayer*

God Machine, The - Scenes from the Second Storey (Fiction Records, 1993) - *Home*

Godflesh - Pure (Earache, 1992)

Green Apple Quick Step - Wonderful Virus (Medicine Label, 1993) - *Dirty Water Ocean*

Green Day - Dookie (Reprise Records, 1994) - *When I Come Around / Basket Case*

Greta - No Biting! (Stardog Records, 1993) – *Fathom*

Guided By Voices - Bee Thousand (Scat Records, 1994)

Happy Mondays - Pills 'n' Thrills and Bellyaches (Factory, 1990) - *Kinki Afro*

Hazel - Toreador of Love (Sub Pop, 1993) - *Day Glo*

Helmet - Meantime (Interscope Records, 1992) – *Unsung*

Hersh, Kristin - Hips and Makers (4AD, 1994) - *Your Ghost*

Hex - Hex (BMG Ariola, 1994) - *1, 2, 3, dobrý deň*

Hole - Live Through This (DGC, 1994) - *Miss World*

House of Pain - House of Pain (Tommy Boy, 1992) - *Jump Around*

Charlatans, The - Some Friendly (Situation Two, 1990) - *The Only One I Know*

Chumbawamba - Anarchy (One Little Indian, 1994) - *Timebomb*

Ice Cube - AmeriKKKa's Most Wanted (Priority Records, 1990) - *Who's the Mack*

Ice-T - O.G. Original Gangster (Rhyme $yndicate Records, 1991)

Ice-T - Home Invasion (Rhyme $yndicate Records, 1993) - *I Ain't New Ta This*

Idaho - Year After Year (Caroline Records, 1993) - *God's Green Earth*

Inspiral Carpets - Life (Mute, 1990)

Inspiral Carpets - Revenge of Goldfish (Mute, 1992) - *Two Worlds Collide*

James - Seven (Fontana, 1992) - *Born of Frustration*

Jamiroquai - Emergency on Planet Earth (Sony Soho Square, 1993) - *Too Young to Die*

Jane's Addiction - Ritual de lo Habitual (Warner Bros. Records, 1990) - *Stop! / Been Caught Stealing*

Jawbox - Novelty (Dischord Records, 1992)

Jawbox - For Your Own Special Sweetheart (Atlantic, 1994) - *Savory*

Jesus and Mary Chain, The - Honey's Dead (Blanco y Negro, 1992) - *Reverence*

Jesus Jones - Doubt (Food Records, 1991) - *Right Here, Right Now*

Jesus Lizard, The - Liar - (Touch and Go, 1992) - *Gladiator*

Jon Spencer Blues Explosion, The - Extra Width (Matador, 1993)

Jon Spencer Blues Explosion, The - Orange (Matador, 1994) – *Bellbottoms*

Judgment Night: Music From The Motion Picture (Immortal Records, 1993) - Faith No More (feat. Boo-Yaa T.R.I.B.E.) - *Another Body Murdered*

Killing Joke - Pandemonium (Butterfly Records, 1994) - *Pandemonium*

King's X - King's X (Atlantic, 1992) - *Black Flag*

King's X - Dogman (Atlantic, 1994) - *Dogman*

Kitchens of Distinction - Strange Free World (One Little Indian, 1991) - *Drive That Fast*

Korn - Korn (Immortal Records, 1994) - *Shoots and Ladders*

Kravitz, Lenny - Mama Said (Virgin Records, 1991) - *Always on the Run*

Kravitz, Lenny - Are You Gonna Go My Way (Virgin Records, 1993) - *Are You Gonna Go My Way*

Kyuss - Blues for the Red Sun (Dali Records, 1992) - *Green Machine*

Kyuss - Welcome to Sky Valley (Elektra, 1994) - *Demon Cleaner*

L7 - Bricks Are Heavy (Slash Records, 1992) - *Pretend We're Dead*

Lagwagon - Trashed (Fat Wreck Chords, 1994) - *Island of Shame*

La's, The - The La's (Go! Discs, 1990) - *There She Goes*

Lanegan, Mark - Whiskey for the Holy Ghost (Sub Pop, 1994) - *House a Home*

Last Action Hero: Music From the Original Motion Picture - (Columbia, 1993)

Leatherface - Minx (Roughneck Recording Company, 1993) - *Do the Right Thing*

Lemonheads, The - It's a Shame About Ray (Atlantic, 1992) - *It's a Shame About Ray / Mrs. Robinson*

Les Thugs - As Happy As Possible (Sub Pop, 1993) - *As Happy As Possible*

Levellers - Levelling the Land (China Records, 1991) - *One Way*

Life of Agony - River Runs Red (Roadrunner Records, 1993) - *This Time*

Live - Throwing Copper (Radioactive, 1994) - *I Alone*

Living Colour - Time's Up (Epic, 1990) - *Type*

Living Colour - Stain (Epic, 1993) – *Nothingness*

LL Cool J - Mama Said Knock You Out (Def Jam Recordings, 1990) - *Mama Said Knock You Out*

Love Battery - Dayglo (Sub Pop, 1992) - *Out of Focus*

Luscious Jackson - In Search of Manny EP (Grand Royal, 1992) - *Daughters of the Kaos*

Lush - Spooky (4AD, 1992) - *For Love*

Machine Head - Burn My Eyes (Roadrunner Records, 1994) - *Old*

Manic Street Preachers - Generation Terrorists (Columbia, 1992) - *Motorcycle Emptiness*

Manic Street Preachers - Gold Against Soul (Columbia, 1993) - *From Despair to Where*

Massive Attack - Blue Lines (Virgin Records, 1991) - *Unfinished Sympathy*

Massive Attack - Protection (Virgin Records, 1994) - *Karmacoma*

MC 900 Ft. Jesus - Welcome to My Dream (I.R.S. Records, 1991) - *Killer Inside Me*

Meat Puppets - Too High to Die (London Records, 1994) - *We Don't Exist*

Mega City Four - Magic Bullets (Big Life, 1993) - *Iron Sky*

Megadeth - Countdown to Extinction (Capitol Records, 1992) - *Symphony of Destruction*

Melvins - Stoner Witch (Atlantic, 1994) - *Revolve*

Mercury Rev - Yerself Is Steam (Mint Films, 1991) - *Car Wash Hair*

Metallica - Metallica (Elektra, 1991) - *Enter Sandman*

Method Man - Tical (Def Jam Recordings, 1994) - *Release Yo' Delf*

Midnight Oil - Blue Sky Mining (CBS, 1990) - *Blue Sky Mine*

Mighty Mighty Bosstones, The - Question the Answers (Mercury, 1994) - *Hell of a Hat*

Mindfunk - Dropped (Megaforce Records, 1993) - *Goddess*

Ministry - Psalm 69 (Sire, 1992) - *Jesus Built My Hotrod*

Mňága a žďorp - Furt rovně! (BMG Ariola, 1992) - *Někdy*

Morphine - Cure for Pain (Rykodisc, 1993) - *Buena*

Morrissey - Bona Drag (His Master's Voice, 1990)

Morrissey - Your Arsenal (His Master's Voice, 1992) - *We Hate It When Our Friends Become Successful*

Morrissey - Vauxhal and I (Parlophone, 1994)

Mother Love Bone - Apple (Polydor, 1990) - *Stardog Champion*

Mudhoney - Piece of Cake (Reprise Records, 1992) - *Suck You Dry*

My Bloody Valentine - Loveless (Creation Records, 1991) - *Soon*

N.W.A. - Niggaz4Life (Ruthless Records, 1991) - *Appetite for Destruction*

Nas - Illmatic (Columbia, 1994) - *Halftime*

Ned's Atomic Dustbin - God Fodder (Furtive, 1991) - *Grey Cell Green*

New Model Army - Impurity (EMI, 1990) - *Purity*

New Model Army - The Love of Hopeless Causes (Epic, 1993) - *Here Comes the War*

New Order - Republic (London Records, 1993) - *Regret*

Nick Cave and the Bad Seeds - The Good Son (Mute, 1990) - *Weeping Song*

Nick Cave and the Bad Seeds - Henry's Dream (Mute, 1992) - *Straight to You*

Nick Cave and the Bad Seeds - Let Love In (Mute, 1994) - *Do You Love Me*

Nine Inch Nails - Broken EP (Nothing Records, 1992) - *Wish*

Nine Inch Nails - The Downward Spiral (Interscope Records, 1994) - *March of the Pigs*

Nirvana - Nevermind (DGC, 1991) - *In Bloom / Smells Like Teen Spirit*

Nirvana - Incesticide (DGC, 1992) - *Sliver*

Nirvana - In Utero (DGC, 1993) - *Heart-Shaped Box*

NOFX - White Trash, Two Heebs and a Bean (Epitaph, 1992) - *Sticking in My Eye*

Noir Désir - Du ciment sous les plaines (Barclay, 1991) - *En Route Pour La Joie*

Nudeswirl - Nudeswirl (Megaforce Records, 1993) - *F-Sharp*

Oasis - Definitely Maybe (Creation Records, 1994) - *Live Forever*

Offspring, The - Smash (Epitaph, 1994) - *Self Esteem*

Onyx - Bacdafucup (JMJ Records, 1993) - *Slam*

Opus III - Mind Fruit (PWL International, 1992) - *It's a Fine Day*

Orb, The - U.F.Orb (Big Life, 1992)

Orbital - Orbital 2 (Internal Records, 1993) - *Halcyon*

Pale Saints - In Ribbons (4AD, 1992) - *Throwing Back the Apples*

Pantera - Vulgar Display of Power (ATCO Records, 1992) - *Mouth for War*

Pavement - Crooked Rain, Crooked Rain (Matador, 1994) - *Cut Your Hair*

Paw - Dragline (A&M Records, 1993) - *Jessie*

Pearl Jam - Ten (Epic, 1991) - *Oceans / Alive*

Pearl Jam - Vitalogy (Epic, 1994) - *Not For You*

Phair, Liz - Exile in Guyville (Matador, 1993)

Phair, Liz - Whip-Smart (Matador, 1994) - *Supernova*

Pharcyde, The - Bizarre Ride II the Pharcyde (Delicious Vinyl, 1992)

Pixies - Trompe Le Monde (4AD, 1991) - *Alec Eiffel*

PJ Harvey - Rid of Me (Island Records, 1993) - *Man-Size*

Polvo - Today's Active Lifestyles (Merge Records, 1993) – *Tilebreaker*

Pop, Iggy - Brick By Brick (Virgin America, 1990) - *Candy*

Pop Will Eat Itself - The Pwei Cure For Sanity (RCA, 1990) - *92 Degrees*

Porno for Pyros - Porno for Pyros (Warner Bros. Records, 1993) - *Pets*

Portishead - Dummy (Go! Beat, 1994) - *Glory Box*

Posies, The - Frosting on the Beater (Geffen Records, 1993) - *I Can Dream All Day*

Priessnitz - Hexe (Bonton, 1994) - *Hlavou dolů*

Primal Scream - Screamadelica (Creation Records, 1991) - *Come Together*

Primal Scream - Give Out But Don't Give Up (Creation Records, 1994) - *Jailbird*

Primus - Sailing the Seas of Cheese (Interscope Records, 1991) – *Jerry Was a Race Car Driver*

Prodigy, The - Experience (XL Recordings, 1992) - *Out of Space*

Prodigy, The - Music for the Jilted Generation (XL Recordings, 1994) - *Voodoo People*

Prong - Cleansing (Epic, 1994) - *Whose Fist Is This Anyway?*

Public Enemy - Fear of a Black Planet (Def Jam, 1990)

Public Enemy - Muse Sick-N-Hour Mess Age (Def Jam Recordings, 1994) - *Give It Up*

Pulp - His 'n' Hers (Island Records, 1994) - *Lipgloss*

Quicksand - Slip (Polydor, 1993) - *Dine Alone*

R.E.M. - Out of Time (Warner Bros. Records, 1991) - *Radio Song / Losing My Religion*

R.E.M. - Automatic for the People (Warner Bros. Records, 1992) - *Drive*

R.E.M. - Monster (Warner Bros. Records, 1994) - *What's the Frequency, Kenneth?*

Radiohead - Pablo Honey (Parlophone, 1993) - *Stop Whispering / Creep*

Rage Against the Machine - Rage Against the Machine (Epic, 1992) - *Freedom / Killing in the Name*

Red Hot Chili Peppers - Blood, Sugar, Sex, Magik (Warner Bros. Records, 1991) - *Suck My Kiss / Give It Away*

Red House Painters - Down Colorful Hill (4AD, 1992) - *24*

Rein Sanction - Mariposa (Sub Pop, 1992) - *Every Color*

Renegade Soundwave - Howyoudoin? (Mute, 1994) - *Renegade Soundwave*

Reverend Horton Heat - Full Custom Gospel Sounds (Sub Pop, 1993) - *Wiggle Stick*

Ride - Nowhere (Creation Records, 1990) - *Vapour Trail*

Rollins Band - Weight (Imago, 1994) - *Liar*

Saint Ettiene - Foxbase Alpha (Heavenly Recordings, 1991) - *Nothing Can Stop Us*

Saint Etienne - So Tough (Heavenly Recordings, 1993)

Samiam - Clumsy (Atlantic, 1994) - *Stepson*

Satchel - EDC (Epic, 1994) - *Mr. Pink*

Screaming Trees - Sweet Oblivion (Epic, 1992) - *Shadow of the Season*

Seaweed - Four (Sub Pop, 1993) - *Kid Candy*

Sebadoh - Bakesale (Sub Pop, 1994) - *Rebound*

Senser - Stacked Up (Ultimate Records, 1994) - *The Key*

Shed Seven - Change Giver (Polydor, 1994) - *Ocean Pie*

Sick of It All - Scratch the Surface (EastWest Records, 1994) - *Step Down*

Singles: Original Motion Picture Soundtrack (Epic Soundtrax, 1992) – Alice In Chains – *Would?*

Siouxsie and the Banshees - Superstition (Polydor, 1991) - *Kiss Them for Me*

Slobodná Európa - Unavení a zničení (Škvrna Records, 1994) - *Podvod*

Slowdive - Souvlaki (Creation Records, 1993) - *Alison*

Smashing Pumpkins, The - Gish (Caroline Records, 1991) - *Siva*

Smashing Pumpkins, The - Siamese Dream (Hut Recordings, 1993) - *Disarm*

Snoop Doggy Dogg - Doggystyle (Death Row Records, 1993) - *Who Am I (What's My Name)?*

So I Married An Axe Murderer: Original Motion Picture Soundtrack (Columbia, 1993)
– The La's – *There She Goes*

Sonic Youth - Goo (DGC, 1990) - *Dirty Boots*

Sonic Youth - Dirty (DGC, 1992) - *Youth Against Fascism*

Soul Asylum - Grave Dancers Union (Columbia, 1992) - *Somebody to Shove / Runaway Train*

Soundgarden - Badmotorfinger (A&M Records, 1991) - *Rusty Cage*

Soundgarden - Superunknown (A&M Records, 1994) - *Fell on Black Days / Black Hole Sun*

Soup Dragons, The - Lovegod (Big Life, 1990) - *I'm Free*

Spin Doctors - Pocket Full of Kryptonite (Epic, 1991) - *Two Princes*

Sponge - Rotting Piñata (Work Records, 1994) - *Plowed*

Stakka Bo - Supermarket (Stockholm Records, 1993) - *Here We Go*

Stereo MC's - Connected (4th & Broadway, 1992) - *Step It Up / Connected*

Stiltskin - Mind's Eye (White Water Records, 1994) - *Footsteps / Inside*

Stone Roses, The - Second Coming (Geffen Records, 1994) - *Love Spreads*

Stone Temple Pilots - Core (Atlantic, 1992) - *Creep / Plush*

Stone Temple Pilots - Purple (Atlantic, 1994) - *Interstate Love Song*

Sublime - 40oz. to Freedom (MCA Records, 1992) - *Date Rape*

Suede - Suede (Nude Records, 1993) - *So Young / Animal Nitrate*

Suede - Dog Man Star (Nude Records, 1994) - *We Are the Pigs*

Sugar - Copper Blue (Rykodisc, 1992) - *If I Can't Change Your Mind*

Sugarcubes - Stick Around for Joy (One Little Indian, 1992) - *Hit*

Sugartooth - Sugartooth (Geffen Records, 1994) - *Sold My Fortune*

Suicidal Tendencies - Art of Rebellion (Epic, 1992) - *I'll Hate You Better*

Sundays, The - Reading, Writing and Arithmetic (Rough Trade, 1990) - *Here's Where the Story Ends*

Sunny Day Real Estate - Diary (Sub Pop, 1994) - *Seven*

Superchunk - On the Mouth (Matador, 1993) - *Precision Auto*

Supersuckers - La Mano Cornuda (Sub Pop, 1994) - *Creepy Jackalope Eye*

Swans - Love of Life (Young God Records, 1992) - *Love of Life*

Swervedriver - Mezcal Head (Creation Records, 1993) - *Last Train to Satansville*

TAD - Inhaler (Giant Records, 1993) – *Leafy Incline*

Tar - Jackson (Amphetamine Reptile, 1991) - *Goethe*

Teenage Fanclub - Bandwagonesque (Creation Records, 1991)

Teenage Fanclub - Thirteen (Creation Records, 1993) - *Hang On*

Temple of the Dog - Temple of the Dog (A&M Records, 1991) - *Hunger Strike*

Terrorvision - How to Make Friends and Influence People (EMI, 1994) – *Oblivion*

Therapy? - Troublegum (A&M Records, 1994) - *Screamager*

Throwing Muses - The Real Ramona (4AD, 1991) - *Counting Backwards*

Toad the Wet Sprocket - Dulcinea (Columbia, 1994) - *Fall Down*

Tool - Undertow (Zoo Entertainment, 1993) - *Sober*

Tribe Called Quest, A - Midnight Marauders (Jive, 1993) - *Award Tour*

Tři sestry - Alkáč je největší kocour aneb několik písní o lásce (Reflex, 1991) - *Zelená*

Type O Negative - Bloody Kisses (Roadrunner Records, 1993) - *Black No. 1*

U2 - Achtung Baby (Island Records, 1991) - *Mysterious Ways*

Ugly Kid Joe - As Ugly as They Wanna Be EP (Stardog Records, 1991) - *Everything About You*

Ugly Kid Joe - America's Least Wanted (Mercury, 1992) - *Cats in the Cradle*

Underworld - Dubnobasswithmyheadman (Junior Boy's Own, 1994) - *Dirty Epic*

Unrest - Perfect Teeth (4AD, 1993) - *Cath Carroll*

Urge Overkill - Stull EP (Touch and Go, 1992) - *Girl, You'll Be a Woman Soon*

Urge Overkill - Saturation (Geffen Records, 1993) - *Sister Havana*

Už jsme doma - Hollywood (Rachot Records, 1993) - *Hollywood*

Velocity Girl - ¡Simpatico! (Sub Pop, 1994) - *Sorry Again*

Verve, The - A Storm in Heaven (Hut Recordings, 1993) - *Slide Away*

Wannadies, The - Be a Girl (Snap Records, 1994) - *You and Me Song*

Warren G - Regulate... G Funk Era (Violator Records, 1994) – *Regulate*

Wedding Present, The - Watusi (Island Records, 1994) - *Yeah Yeah Yeah Yeah Yeah*

Ween - Chocolate and Cheese (Elektra, 1994) - *Voodoo Lady*

Weezer - Blue Album (DGC, 1994) - *Buddy Holly*

Weller, Paul - Wild Wood (Go! Discs, 1993) - *Wild Wood*

White Zombie - La Sexorcisto: Devil Music Vol. 1 (Geffen Records, 1992)

Wu-Tang Clan - Enter the Wu-Tang (36 Chambers) (Loud Records, 1993) - *C.R.E.A.M.*

Young, Neil - Harvest Moon (Reprise Records, 1992) - *Harvest Moon*

Bibliography and additional resources

Albini, S. (1993). The Problem with Music. *The Baffler.* http://thebaffler.com/salvos/the-problem-with-music

Apfelová, S. (2011). *Ženy - inštrumentalistky v rockovej hudbe.* Bakalárska práca, FFUK Bratislava, Katedra hudobnej vedy

Aston, M. (2013). *Facing the Other Way: The Story of 4AD.* The Friday Project

Azzerad, M. (1994). *Come As You Are: The Story of Nirvana.* Three Rivers Press

Azzerad, M. (2001). *Our Band Could Be Your Life: Scenes from the American Indie Underground 1981-1991.* Little, Brown and Company

Beaumont, M. (2012). Best Ever Year For Music? I'm Going With 1992. *NME.* http://www.nme.com/blogs/nme-blogs/best-ever-year-for-music-im-going-with-1992

Buhrmester, J. (2010). The Oral History of Epitaph Records. *SPIN.* http://www.spin.com/2010/10/oral-history-epitaph-records/

DeCurtis, A. (1992). 1992: The Year in Music. *Rolling Stone.* http://www.rollingstone.com/music/news/the-year-in-music-19921210

Deusner, S. M. (2013). Facing the Other Way: The Story of 4AD. *Pitchfork,* http://pitchfork.com/features/paper-trail/9281-facing-the-other-way-the-story-of-4ad/

Dilworth, J. (2015). Daniel Miller: 'I was determined to make Mute a success'. *[PIAS]*. http://www.pias.com/blog/daniel-miller-determined-make-mute-success/

Fletcher, T. (2013). *Perfect Circle: The Story of R.E.M.*. Omnibus Press

Goldfein, J. (1999). Touch and Go v. The Buttholes. *Chicago Reader.* http://www.chicagoreader.com/chicago/touch-and-go-v-the-buttholes/Content?oid=898923

Ham, R. (2015). Sights Unheard: SNUB TV. *Paste Magazine.* https://www.pastemagazine.com/articles/2015/02/sights-unheard-snub-tv.html

Hann, M. (2013). Sub Pop: 25 years of underground rock. *The Guardian.* https://www.theguardian.com/music/2013/jul/04/sub-pop-25-years-underground-rock

Harris, J. (2005). Remember the First Time. *The Guardian.* https://www.theguardian.com/music/2005/aug/12/pulp.popandrock

Hayden, S. (2010). Whatever Happened To Alternative Nation? *The A.V. Club.* http://www.avclub.com/features/whatever-happened-to-alternative-nation/

Heller, J. (2014). Fear Of A Punk Decade. *The A.V. Club.* http://www.avclub.com/features/fear-of-a-punk-decade/

Herzog, K. (2012). 'Experiencing Nirvana': Sub Pop Co-Founder Revisits Defining 1989 Tour. *SPIN.* http://www.spin.com/2012/11/experiencing-nirvana-ebook-kurt-cobain-pavitt-grunge-europe/

Mapes, J. (2014). Why 1993 Was the Best Musical Year of the '90s. *Billboard*. http://www.billboard.com/articles/columns/pop-shop/6273797/1993-best-musical-year-1990s

Mellor, J. C. (2010-2016). 1990-1994 Rock Music Timeline. *Rock Music Timeline*. http://www.rockmusictimeline.com/1990s.html

Myers, B. (2009). Label of Love: Touch and Go. *The Guardian*. https://www.theguardian.com/music/2009/apr/20/label-love-touch-go

Nickson, Ch. (2015). The History of Britpop. *Ministry of Rock*. http://www.ministryofrock.co.uk/britpop.html

Partridge, K. (2014). Why 1990 Was the Best Musical Year of the '90s. *Billboard*. http://www.billboard.com/articles/columns/pop-shop/6273788/1990-best-musical-1990s

Pearl Jam, Crowe, C. (2011). *Pearl Jam Twenty*. Simon & Schuster

Rabin, N. (2011). My Favourite Music Year - 1994. *The A.V. Club*. http://www.avclub.com/article/1994-54854

Rabin, N. (2012). Hip-Hop And You Do Stop. *The A.V. Club*. http://www.avclub.com/features/hip-hop-and-you-do-stop/

Ramirez, A. J. (2011). A Landmark Year for Rock Albums. *PopMatters*. http://www.popmatters.com/post/136563-1991-a-landmark-year-for-rock-albums/

Rosenthal, E. (2014). Why 1994 Was the Best Musical Year of the '90s. *Billboard*. http://www.billboard.com/articles/columns/pop-shop/6273800/1994-best-musical-year-1990s

Ryan, K. (2011). My Favourite Music Year - 1993. *The A.V. Club.* http://www.avclub.com/article/1993-61084

Schuftan, C. (2012). *Entertain Us: The Rise and Fall of Alternative Rock in the Nineties.* HarperCollins Publishers

Schuftan, C. (2014). Love in the Nineties. *ABC – Australian Broadcasting Corporation.* http://www.abc.net.au/radionational/programs/intothemusic/features/love-in-the-nineties/

Stevens, A. (2003). Leave Them All Behind - 'Shoegazing' and British indie music in the 1990s. *A.M. Magazine.* http://www.3ammagazine.com/musicarchives/2003/jan/shoegazing.html

Transpontine, N. (2014). Revolt of the Ravers – The Movement against the Criminal Justice Act in Britain 1993-95. *Datacide Magazine.* https://datacide-magazine.com/revolt-of-the-ravers-the-movement-against-the-criminal-justice-act-in-britain-1993-95/

Unterberger, A. (2014). Why 1991 Was the Best Musical Year of the '90s. *Billboard.* http://www.billboard.com/articles/columns/pop-shop/6273792/1991-best-musical-year-1990s

Wragg, J. (2014). Tracing the Roots of Trip Hop: How One City's History Influenced a Global Genre. *Academia.edu.* http://www.academia.edu/10235810/Tracing_the_Roots_of_Trip_Hop_How_One_City_s_History_Influenced_a_Global_Genre

Made in United States
North Haven, CT
08 May 2023

36360012R00141